THE SOCIAL SECURITY BENEFITS HANDBOOK

Third Edition

Stanley A. Tomkiel III
Attorney at Law

SPHINX® PUBLISHING
AN IMPRINT OF SOURCEBOOKS, INC.®
NAPERVILLE, ILLINOIS
www.SphinxLegal.com

Third Edition, 2001
Third Printing, May, 2002

Published by: **Sphinx® Publishing, An Imprint of Sourcebooks, Inc.®**

Naperville Office
P.O. Box 4410
Naperville, Illinois 60567-4410
630-961-3900
Fax: 630-961-2168
www.sourcebooks.com
www.SphinxLegal.com

This publication is designed to provide accurate and authoritative information in regard to the subject matter covered. It is sold with the understanding that the publisher is not engaged in rendering legal, accounting, or other professional service. If legal advice or other expert assistance is required, the services of a competent professional person should be sought.

From a Declaration of Principles Jointly Adopted by a Committee of the American Bar Association and a Committee of Publishers and Associations

This product is not a substitute for legal advice.

Disclaimer required by Texas statutes

Library of Congress Cataloging-in-Publication Data
Tomkiel, Stanley A.
    The social security benefits handbook / Stanley A. Tomkiel III.--3rd ed.
        p. cm. -- (Legal survival guides)
    Includes index.
    ISBN 1-57248-168-4
    1. Social security--Law and legislation--United States--Popular works. I. Title. II. Series.
KF3650 .T65 2001
344.73'023--dc21
                                                                    2001041176

Printed and bound in the United States of America.

BG Paperback — 10 9 8 7 6 5 4 3

CONTENTS

INTRODUCTION

THE PURPOSE AND SCOPE OF THE SOCIAL SECURITY BENEFITS HANDBOOK

I have been involved with Social Security for many years, first as a claims representative for the Social Security Administration (SSA) and now as a private attorney. Many things have changed over the years but some things have not. Confusion, misunderstanding, and frustration seem to be constants for people seeking to get accurate and specific information about Social Security benefits quickly and easily.

Although it is the goal of the SSA to provide the public with information and advice about the programs it administers, the realities are such that, despite its best efforts, many people find it difficult to get the particular information they need, or to even know what they need. And some things are purposely not disseminated, such as SSA's guidelines on accepting compromise offers to settle overpayments (see Section (Sec.) 1110), your right to file only for Medicare without filing for retirement benefits (see Sec. 404.3—sometimes this is beneficial), or your option to pro-rate work deductions instead of full withholding of benefits. (see Sec. 803.1.)

The system is complex, with many variables. A bare statement of rules, without practical examples of how they apply in specific cases, is inadequate. Frequently, generalizations are not helpful. Some people who take the common advice to file for benefits three months in advance of retirement may actually lose some benefits. (see Sec. 404.2.) Even though this rule of thumb applies in many cases, it is small consolation if you lose thousands of dollars by following it.

Sometimes the realities of how the system works do not fit in with the official policy of how it should work. SSA does not advertise its shortcomings. It does an admirable job, usually. But sometimes checks don't come (see Sec. 1011), people have to wait for hours to speak with someone (see Sec. 105), interviewers are incompetent or inexperienced, or Social Security wants erroneously paid benefits to be returned. (see Chapter 11.) These things happen, certainly in only a relatively small number of cases, but if yours is one of them, you need some practical advice. You are not likely to find it in a pamphlet.

I have designed this handbook to give you all the major rules about Social Security benefits:

- to show you how they work in particular cases;

- to highlight the situations that can make a dollars and cents difference, or are often misunderstood; and

- to give you the benefit of my practical experience in dealing with thousands of cases as both a "front line"

Social Security official and as a private attorney representing claimants before the Administration.

The handbook contains fourteen chapters by topic, divided into more than two hundred numbered and captioned sections for easy access to specific information, with numerous cross-references and examples for better understanding. It covers just about everything you need to know about monthly benefits.

I hope that my efforts will save you time, frustration, and perhaps even some money. I know that the *Social Security Benefits Handbook* will give you a unique understanding and serve as a handy reference source for accurate, substantial, and practical knowledge about this very important part of your life.

If you have any specific questions on Social Security benefits, you can contact the author through his website at:

http://www.SocialSecurityConsultant.com

THE SOCIAL SECURITY ADMINISTRATION 1

IN GENERAL

Section 101

The Social Security Administration (SSA) is the branch of the Federal government that has the duty of administering several provisions of the Social Security Act. SSA was under the jurisdiction of the Department of Health and Human Services until March 1995, when it became an independent agency.

The Social Security Act provides for the payment of monthly benefits to retired and disabled workers and their dependents and to certain survivors of covered workers who are deceased. Social Security also provides for Medicare and other programs such as Supplemental Security Income and Black Lung benefits. The benefits referred to as Social Security benefits, however, are those monthly benefits payable to retired workers, disabled workers, and the survivors of covered workers.

Because regular Social Security benefits are based on the earnings of covered workers, SSA also keeps track of the earnings of almost all American workers.

There are presently approximately forty-nine million people throughout the United States who receive monthly checks from SSA and there are approximately 153 million covered workers whose wages are recorded by SSA. SSA is one of the largest government agencies.

SSA is divided into many different bureaus and branches to accomplish all its duties. The main offices are located in Baltimore, Maryland. The entire United States is divided up by SSA into districts, each of which has its own District Office. Many of these District Offices also have branch offices. There are seven hundred district and branch offices throughout the nation. The District Office is designed to handle all contact with members of the public. Normally, most dealings you will have with SSA will be done through your local District Office.

This chapter will discuss the different bureaus and their general functions and will discuss the different types of District Office employees with whom you will come in contact.

INTERNAL OFFICES

Section 102

SSA makes contact with members of the public through District Offices and Teleservice Centers. (see Secs. 103 and 105 below.) However, much of the work of SSA is done by people in offices that have no contact with the public. We will discuss some of these major offices that the public never sees. These are referred to as *internal offices*.

Central Office (CO)

The main office of SSA is called the *Central Office*. It is the headquarters of SSA and is located in Baltimore. The Central

Office issues all regulations and instruction to the District Offices. It interprets the law and issues policy statements.

Office of Central Records Operations (OCRO)

This office deals with the huge volume of information necessary to perform the duties of SSA. Its main functions include the assigning of Social Security numbers to workers, keeping track of changes of names on Social Security records, and maintaining the records of earnings reported by employers for each individual Social Security number. This office is also located in Baltimore. When a person files a claim for Social Security benefits, the District Office where the claim is being handled must contact the Office of Central Records Operations to obtain the earnings record of the worker.

Program Service Centers (PSC)

There are six Program Service Centers located throughout the United States. These offices process claims that cannot be processed by the District Office. They also process reinstatement of benefits after they have been suspended or terminated.

After a claim has been processed in a district office it is sent to the Program Service Center for storage and further processing. The claims folders are generally assigned to the different program service centers based on the Social Security number of the wage earner on whose earnings the claim is based. The names and addresses of the different program service centers, along with the breakdown of their claims numbers is listed in Appendix 8.

Sometimes the Program Service Center has direct contact with beneficiaries. They handle such things as student reports, annual report of earnings and overpayment notices. Any information requested from a Program Service Center can be returned directly or can be returned through a local District Office, whichever you prefer.

Office of Disability Operations (ODO)

This office is similar to a Program Service Center, but it handles cases based on disability benefits. If a worker who is disabled is age fifty-nine or older, his file is maintained in the Program Service Center instead of the Office of Disability Operations.

When the person turns sixty-five his disability benefit is automatically converted to a retirement benefit by the Program Service Center. This conversion to a retirement benefit is only a technicality; the amount of the benefit does not change. The files of disabled workers younger than fifty-nine are kept in the Office of Disability Operations. This office is also located in Baltimore.

Division of International Operations (DIO)

This office is similar to a Program Service Center, but it covers cases where beneficiaries reside outside of the United States. It is also located in Baltimore.

Regional Offices (RO)

The entire United States is divided into ten regions by SSA. Each region has a Regional Office which deals directly with the Central Office and then deals with the local District Offices within the region. An individual District Office in the region does not have direct contact with Central Office. Instead it deals through the Regional Office. The Regional Office is staffed with experts in all areas of Social Security.

Regional offices also review the District Offices to make sure that they are applying the rules and regulations of Social Security consistently.

TELEPHONE SERVICES

Section 103

SSA has set up special centers designed to handle telephone inquiries from members of the public. These are called Teleservice Centers (TSC). They are designed to take the burden of voluminous phone calls away from the District Office. The nationwide toll free number is 800-772-1213. Service representatives handle calls from 7:00 a.m. to 7:00 p.m. Pre-recorded information and services are available after hours. Hearing impaired callers with TDD equipment can call 800-325-0778 between 7:00 a.m. and 7:00 p.m. Medicare information is available from 8:00 a.m. to 8:00 p.m. Eastern time at 800-638-6833.

The Teleservice Centers are staffed by Service Representatives. (see Sec. 105.) They have computer terminals available to obtain the computer records of all beneficiaries who have been established on the computer. (see Sec. 104.) They are able to handle changes of address and reports of missing checks. If a claim has been recently filed and has not yet been set up on the computer system, you will be referred to the local District Office where the claim is being handled. That phone number was given to you at the time you filed your initial application on the receipt form that Social Security gives everyone who files a claim.

The Teleservice Centers can also provide general information about Social Security, although it is recommended that you speak with a Claims Representative if the question is out of the ordinary or is complex.

District Office Telephone Service

Many District Offices have telephone service available to file claims, report changes of address or missing checks, and obtain information regarding Social Security. Almost all business you may have with the Social Security office can be handled over the telephone. You can even file a claim on the phone.

Many District Offices have what are referred to as teleclaims units. These units are staffed by Claims Representatives who will obtain the necessary information from you over the phone, complete the application form, and mail it to you for your review and signature.

It is against the policy of many Social Security offices to send out blank application forms. If you call them up to file a claim, you will have to give the information over the phone, so that the Claims Representative can properly fill out the application. This is done to ensure that there is no misunderstanding of information, and that all the information and required evidence is obtained.

❐ Section 103.1 Internet Website

The Social Security Administration publishes an impressive website on the Internet located at: **http://www.ssa.gov**. It is relatively user-friendly, but contains so much information that a visitor may become overwhelmed.

Nevertheless, it has very useful features. A benefits calculator that can give an estimate of your benefit based on various earnings assumptions; a request link to obtain your Social Security earnings record (which is mailed to you); and even an on-line application form that can be electronically submitted. However, you must print out the form, sign it and mail the signed document to SSA. You may also request a Medicare replacement card as well as a Social Security card.

There are links to official statutes and regulations, as well as links to several other federal government websites. The site is frequently up-dated with current relevant news items.

COMPUTER SYSTEM

Section 104

SSADARS (pronounced "SAY-DARS") is the basic computer system of SSA. It links all District Offices nationwide. It allows personnel in the local District Office to make computer inputs to establish claims on the rolls and to make any necessary changes, such as change of address or reports of missing checks.

Records of individual beneficiaries are stored on the computer system. Such things as payment amounts, addresses, beneficiaries on record, and so forth, may be obtained from the computer. All District Offices have on-line terminals to the SSADARS. This means that they can obtain the information almost immediately. Unfortunately, no computer system is perfect and sometimes the system is down. When this happens the personnel in the District Office cannot get the information immediately.

When claims can be processed through the SSADARS, the time frames for processing are greatly reduced. Unfortunately, not all claims can be processed this way, but the majority can.

For claims that cannot go through the system, manual processing at a Program Service Center is required. (see Sec. 106.) This adds significantly to the time required for processing. A claim going through the computer system can take as little as fifteen days. A claim going through manual processing may take up to three months or more.

The District Office (DO)

Section 105

The entire United States is divided geographically by SSA into many hundreds of districts. There are over 1,100 district and branch offices throughout the United States. Each district or branch office is responsible for dealing with all members of the public who reside in that district.

Any business you may have to conduct with SSA will be done through your local District Office. You may determine where your District Office is located by looking in the telephone book under United States Government, Social Security Administration. You may deal with any District Office you prefer. If another District Office is more convenient than your own local District Office, you may ask that your case be handled at the other one.

District Offices are open during regular business hours. The exact times of opening and closing change from one office to another. Some offices open at 8:00 a.m. and close at 4:30 p.m. Other offices open at 8:30 a.m. and close at 5:00 p.m. Most of your business with Social Security can be conducted over the telephone without having to go in person to the District Office. (see Sec. 103.)

If you wish to visit your district office in person, you cannot usually make an appointment. Visitors at the district office are taken on a first-come, first-served basis.

Best Times to Visit the District Office

Sometimes you can visit a District Office and be served immediately. Other times you may have to wait for an hour or more. It all depends on how crowded the office is when you get there. The volume of visitors to District Offices usually follows a pattern, and if you go at a time when it is not crowded you will be served more promptly.

Generally speaking, you are better off going to your District Office towards the end of a month. The first seven to ten days are usually the busiest in a District Office. It is at these times that you may encounter a wait of an hour or more. The reason is that most Social Security checks are paid on the third day of the month. (see Sec. 1003.) Supplemental Security Income checks (see Sec. 1401) are paid on the first day of the month. Each month, there are many people who do not receive their checks, or have had them stolen. Therefore, district offices are usually crowded during the first week to ten days of any given month.

Generally, the second half of the week is less busy than the first. Mondays are usually very busy, whereas Fridays are slow.

The District Offices are busy during lunchtime. This is because many people who work go there at their own lunchtime, and also because Social Security employees have to eat, too. Interviewers at the Social Security office have staggered lunch hours so that at least half of them will be on duty during this time. However, because the other half is out to lunch, the lines can grow, and you may encounter delays.

Likewise, the employees at the District Office take coffee breaks. They receive a fifteen-minute coffee break in the afternoon. Again, these breaks are staggered, but at around 10:00 a.m. and 3:00 p.m., half of the interviewers are on their coffee breaks.

Processing Units

The business handled by the District Office is divided into different units. Each unit is staffed by one or more employees. Among interviewers, the basic division is between claims units and service units. Claims units handle initial applications and the more complex areas of Social Security rules. They are staffed by Claims Representatives.

The service units handle what are referred to as *post-entitlement* issues. These are the events that occur after you have become entitled to checks, such as changes of address, reports of missing checks, annual reports of earnings, and so forth. Service units are staffed by Service Representatives. A Service Representative is not able to handle an initial claim.

Generally, there is a special unit set up in each District Office to handle disability related cases, and a special unit for Supplemental Security Income cases. (see Sec. 1401.) In larger offices the work is further divided among the Claims Representatives and Service Representatives based on an alphabetical breakdown.

Each Claims Representative and Service Representative will be assigned a certain part of the alphabet and the cases of all persons with names that fall within that part of the alphabet will be assigned to that particular Claims Representative or Service Representative. That worker will handle the paper work for the claim, but may interview people regardless of the alphabetical breakdown.

The different Claims Representatives and Service Representatives are periodically re-assigned to different alphabetical breakdowns, so do not be surprised to find that a different Claims Representative will be handling your case a few months later.

The different types of employees that you come in contact with at the local District Office will be discussed later in this chapter.

In addition to District Offices, the Social Security Administration also sets up Branch Offices and contact stations. The Branch Office is a smaller version of the District Office and comes under its jurisdiction. It is staffed with the same types of employees found in the District Office. The manager of a Branch Office reports to the manager of the District Office with which it is associated.

The contact station is not a regular office. It is simply a place where a Field Representative or a Claims Representative goes on a periodic basis to service people in outlying areas. They are usually set up in areas where the jurisdiction of the District Office is large. The Field Representative will go to the contact station at set times, such as the third Tuesday of the month, for example. All paper work is taken back to the District Office and processed there by the regular personnel according to the alphabetical breakdown.

If you live far from your local District Office, you should find out if a contact station is set up closer to you and when the

Social Security representative will be there. Contact Stations are commonly established in municipal buildings or senior citizen centers.

District Office Personnel In General

Each District Office is staffed with many types of employees, each one handling specific functions. Every District Office has a district manager, who is the highest authority in the office. The district manager is not usually involved with the technical aspects of Social Security, deciding claims. His or her duties are basically administrative, for example maintaining personnel records and making sure the office work moves along quickly.

He or she also deals with Congressmen and Senators who make inquiries on behalf of their constituents. (see Sec. 1014.) The district manager is the person to contact in the District Office if you wish to praise a particular employee for a job well done or to complain about an employee for poor service.

Generally, the district manager does not deal with the public on a regular basis. The employees who deal with the public regularly are Claims Representatives, Service Representatives, Field Representatives, and the receptionist. In addition to these employees who have public contact, there are supervisors, clericals, and technical employees who deal with the paper work and the computers.

If you visit your local Social Security office and have to wait because all the interviewers are tied up interviewing people, you may see a number of employees sitting at desks, and not interviewing anyone. Do not be upset, these are probably the non-interviewing personnel.

The Receptionist

When you go to your District Office, you will be greeted at the front desk by the receptionist. The receptionist will ask your name and a few questions to determine the nature of your visit. It is the receptionists job to determine which employee should service you. At the District Office, different types of business are handled by different employees.

In addition to the reception duties, the receptionist usually handles matters dealing with Social Security numbers, such as assigning new numbers or changing your name for the Social Security records. The receptionist has little training other than that and it is not a good idea to take advice on anything else from the receptionist. Some overzealous receptionists have been known to give erroneous information about Social Security matters. It is wise to take your advice only from a Claims or Service Representative.

After taking your name and determining the nature of your visit, the receptionist will generally ask you to be seated and will assign you to the next available representative who handles your type of case. It is possible that other persons who have arrived after you will be taken care of first because a representative who handles their type of business becomes available before a representative who handles your type of business.

The Claims Representative (CR)

The Claims Representative position is perhaps the single most important position in the entire Social Security organization. It is the responsibility of the Claims Representative to be knowledgeable about all aspects of the Social Security regulations.

The duty of the Claims Representative is two fold. One aspect is to represent the SSA, and the other aspect is to assist claimants who are making claims for benefits under the Social Security program. The major responsibility of the Claims Representative, of course, has to do with initial claims for benefits. The Claims Representative interviews a prospective claimant, determines the type of claim he or she should be making, and completes the appropriate claims forms.

The Claims Representative also determines what documents, evidence, or other information is required to successfully prosecute the claim, and advises the claimant accordingly. The Claims Representative takes steps to obtain the necessary information or documents. Additionally, on many of these initial claims, the Claims Representative makes the decision to pay or to deny the claim.

In addition to these claims duties, the Claims Representative is responsible for making determinations relating to representative payees (see Sec. 1414) for incompetent beneficiaries; for making determinations of the proper amount of wages which are subject to Social Security; and for making recommendations about whether overpayments may be waived in particular cases.

It is also the duty of the Claims Representative to provide the public with information about Social Security rules, regulations, and procedures.

In theory, the Claims Representative knows everything about all aspects of Social Security. This knowledge is not gained in a short period of time, however, and in a given District Office there will be Claims Representatives with varying degrees of experience.

When a person becomes a Claims Representative, he or she is considered to be a trainee for three years in that position because it takes at least that long to get a good working knowledge of all the rules and regulations involved with the job. It takes at least another year of experience to become fully versed in all the aspects of Social Security for which the Claims Representative is responsible.

The majority of seasoned Claims Representatives are thoroughly knowledgeable professionals who are well versed in all aspects of Social Security law and regulations. There are some exceptions to that general statement. Because of the very complex and technical nature of the area, a number of Claims Representatives, even though they are on the job for many years, are still not thoroughly competent. (Just as there are incompetent doctors and lawyers, there are incompetent Claims Representatives.)

If you believe that the Claims Representative with whom you are dealing is giving you erroneous or inaccurate information, ask him to show you the authority for his statement in the program operations manual. (see Sec. 106.) If you are still not satisfied, you should then ask to speak to an operations supervisor to double check.

The Service Representative (SR)

As noted above, there are two basic types of employees who interview the public—Claims Representatives and Service Representatives. The Claims Representative is discussed above. Basically, the Service Representative deals with *post-entitlement* aspects of Social Security. Post-entitlement has to do with things that affect people who are already receiving benefits.

Changes of address, reports of missing checks, annual report of earnings, refunds of overpayments, and Medicare claims are the most common things with which the Service Representative deals. These employees are also well versed in the *retirement test*, also known as the earnings limitations. The retirement test is used to determine how earnings affect benefits. This is fully discussed in Chapter 8.

Service Representatives do not handle claims, payee determinations, changes to the earnings record, or other complex areas of Social Security.

The workload in a District Office is divided among the Service Representatives according to an alphabetical breakdown. Beneficiaries are assigned to Service Representatives based on their last names. For example, a Service Representative may be assigned the letters "A" through "E." If your name begins with an "A" through an "E," your case will be assigned to that Service Representative.

The Service Representatives are periodically re-assigned to different alphabetical breakdowns. You may not have the same Service Representative assigned to your case each time you go to the District Office. The alphabetical breakdowns are used only for paper work processing. Interviewers may be assigned without regard to alphabetical breakdowns if this is required to avoid delays.

The job of the Service Representative requires a thorough knowledge of complicated rules and procedures. Most Service

Representatives are very competent. Unfortunately, some are not. If you question the accuracy of information or advice from a Service Representative, you should ask him or her to show you the authority for the information in the claims manual or programs operations manual. (see Sec. 106.) If you are still not satisfied, you may ask to speak to an operations supervisor.

The Field Representative (FR)

Each District and Branch Office has at least one Field Representative. A Field Representative is basically a Claims Representative who goes out of the office when the need arises. This usually occurs when a claimant or beneficiary is homebound or in the hospital.

The Field Representative makes speeches before groups and visits contact stations. The Field Representative does not usually process the paper work. Instead, he or she brings it back to the District Office where it is assigned to the appropriate Claims Representative or Service Representative according to the alphabetical breakdown, as discussed above.

If you belong to a group or an organization that would like to hear a speaker on Social Security matters, you can call your local District Office and ask the Field Representative to make a speech. Field Representatives frequently work at night and on weekends for these purposes. The Field Representative's broad-based knowledge is usually sufficient to answer all general questions.

THE PROGRAMS OPERATIONS MANUAL SYSTEM (POMS)

Section 106

The Programs Operations Manual System (POMS) is the rulebook used by all District Office personnel. These manuals are issued by the Central Office and provide the working rules and interpretations of the law and regulations. The official regulations of SSA, published in the Federal Register and available in law libraries, are almost never used by the personnel in the District Offices. Instead, they rely almost exclusively upon the POMS. The POMS is available in every District Office for review by members of the public. It is also available online at the SSA website: **http://www.ssa.gov**. Look for "SSA Program Rules—Other Reference Materials."

Generally, the policy of the Social Security office is to require an interviewer to be present while a member of the public reviews the POMS. This is required because much of the language is written in bureaucratic shorthand which can be meaningless to you. A Claims or Service Representative will be required to interpret this bureaucratic language.

The POMS is the "Bible" of Social Security, and all decisions must be founded upon the provisions contained in these manuals. If you doubt the accuracy of information given to you by any Social Security interviewer, you should ask to see where it is stated in the POMS. The interviewer should be able to locate the pertinent section to show you in black and white.

ELIGIBILITY REQUIREMENTS 2

In General

Section 201

The Social Security Act provides for the payment of many different types of benefits. Each type of benefit has specific eligibility requirements that a claimant must meet in order to receive the benefit. The requirements of the different types of benefits are stated in the following sections. Once a person becomes entitled to a benefit, the benefit may not be paid because earnings are in excess of the applicable limits, or for other reasons.

This chapter deals only with the basic eligibility requirements. Earnings as they affect the payment of benefits will be discussed in Chapter 8, EARNINGS LIMITATIONS.

Also, almost all benefits require an application to be filed by the claimant. Application requirements are discussed in full in Chapter 4.

Each type of benefit requires that the worker on whose record the benefits are based have what is called an *insured status*. This means that he or she must have enough work credits.

There are different kinds of insured status. Some require more work than others. These different types of insured status will be discussed in detail in Chapter 6. This chapter will deal with eligibility requirements other than the application requirements and the insured status requirement in detail.

The amount of the actual benefit the beneficiary will receive will be discussed in detail in Chapter 7, BENEFIT AMOUNTS.

The benefits usually referred to as Social Security benefits are provided under the basic programs of the Social Security Act. These are Retirement Insurance, Survivors Insurance, Disability Insurance, and Health Insurance.

Disabled and retired workers, their spouses, and their children, are paid monthly benefits if they meet the eligibility requirements discussed in this chapter. Under survivors insurance, widows and young children are paid monthly benefits if they meet the eligibility requirements discussed in this chapter. Benefits are also payable to some divorced spouses and divorced widows and to some parents of covered workers.

There are many different kinds of monthly benefits. We have categorized fifteen different types of benefits in this chapter. Eligibility requirements for each are listed separately.

In addition to monthly benefits, the Social Security Act also provides for Medicare. This is officially called Health Insurance and has two parts—Hospital Insurance and Medical Insurance. This is discussed more fully in Chapter 12, MEDICARE. We list the eligibility requirements in this chapter.

We do not discuss eligibility requirements for other programs which are administered by Social Security such as Supplemental Security Income (see Sec. 1401) or Black Lung benefits. (see Sec. 1402.) We deal only with the regular Social Security benefits in this chapter.

RETIREMENT BENEFITS

Section 202

Other Names: Old Age Insurance Benefits; Retirement Insurance Benefits

Beneficiary Identification Code: A (see Sec. 1407.)

Requirements:

1. You are at least sixty-two throughout the month (see Sec. 207.4);

2. you have enough work covered by Social Security to be "fully insured" (see Sec. 602);and

3. you file an application (see Chapter 4).

Benefit Amount: One hundred percent of the Primary Insurance Amount (see Sec. 702.1) at Full Retirement Age; reduced for age before Full Retirement Age. (See Chapter 7 for a full discussion.)

Termination: Entitlement ends with the month before the month of death. (see Sec. 1009.)

DISABILITY BENEFITS

Section 203

Other Names: Disability Insurance Benefits; Disabled Worker Benefits

Beneficiary Identification Code: HA (see Sec. 1407.)

Requirements:

1. You are under Full Retirement Age (a full unreduced retirement benefit is paid at Full Retirement Age instead of disability benefits, even if you are disabled);
2. you have enough work covered by Social Security to meet the special disability insured status (see Sec. 604);
3. you file an application (see Chapter 4);
4. you are totally disabled (see Sec. 502); and
5. you have been totally disabled for at least five months (see Sec. 507).

Benefit Amount: One hundred percent of the Primary Insurance Amount (see Sec. 702.1) not reduced for age. (See Chapter 7 for a full discussion of computations of benefits, and see Sections 511 and 512 for the effect of workers compensation benefits or other disability benefits. The disability benefit is subject to offset in some cases.)

Termination: Entitlement ends with:

1. the month before you turn Full Retirement Age (you are automatically switched to Retirement benefits);
2. the second month after the disability ceases (see Sec. 513); or
3. the month before the month of death (see Sec. 1009).

SPOUSE'S BENEFITS

Section 204

❏ Section 204.1 Spouse's Benefits: Age Sixty-two and Older

Other Names: Wife's Benefits; Husband's Benefits (depending on sex); Aged Spouse; Aged Wife; Aged Husband

Beneficiary Identification Code: B (or HB if the worker received disability benefits) (*see Sec. 1407.*)

Requirements:

1. You are the wife or husband of a worker entitled to retirement or disability benefits. Note: the marriage may be "deemed valid" by SSA even if it is not legally recognized (see Sec. 207.5);

2. your marriage lasted for at least one year (see Sec. 207.6 for exceptions to this requirement);

3. you are at least sixty-two throughout the month (see Sec. 207.4);

4. you file an application (see Chapter 4); and

5. you are not entitled to a higher retirement or disability benefit on your own earnings record. [You may be entitled to some spouse's benefits even if you are entitled on your own record, if your benefit is lower than one half of your spouse's Primary Insurance Amount (see Sec. 302).]

Benefit Amount: One half of your spouse's Primary Insurance Amount (see Sec. 702.1) at Full Retirement Age reduced for age before Full Retirement Age (see Sec. 703.1) unless you have a child in your care (see Sec. 207.8);

reduced by your own benefit (see Sec. 302); and subject to the family maximum. (See Chapter 7 for a full discussion.)

Termination: Entitlement ends with:

1. the month before you become entitled to a higher benefit on your own account (see Sec. 302);

2. the month before you become divorced (you may be able to switch over to divorced spouse's benefit—Sec. 204.2);

3. the month before the spouse on whose earnings you receive benefits dies or is no longer disabled [in the event of death you may switch to a widow(er)'s benefit (see Sec. 204.4 for requirements and see Sec. 405 for automatic conversion from spouse's to widow(er)'s benefits)];

4. if your benefits are based on a "deemed" marriage, (see Sec. 207.5), the month before you marry someone else or the legal wife of the worker becomes entitled on his account; or

5. the month before the month of death (see Sec. 1009).

Other: Spouse's benefits are now gender neutral. You may be eligible either as the husband or the wife of the worker. Whenever the term wife's benefits is used in this book, you may substitute husband's benefits if applicable.

❒ Sec. 204.2 Spouse's Benefits: With Child in Care

Other Names: Young Wife; Young Husband; Young Spouse

Beneficiary Identification Code: B2 (or HB2 if the worker receives disability benefits) (see Sec. 1407.)

Requirements: The requirements are the same as an aged spouse; (see Sec. 204.1), with one exception. You may collect at any age as long as you have a child of the worker in your care (see Sec. 207.8) who is entitled to child benefits on the worker's account and who is either under age sixteen or a disabled child of any age for whom you are rendering substantial personal services. (See Secs. 205.1-205.4 for who qualifies as a child.)

Benefit Amount: Fifty percent of the spouse's Primary Insurance Amount. (see Sec. 702.) There is no reduction for being under Full Retirement Age. The benefit is subject to reduction for the family maximum. (See Chapter 7 for a full discussion of computations.)

Termination: Occurs the same as for aged spouse's benefits (see Sec. 204.1), and the month before the month the youngest child turns sixteen. (see Sec. 207.8.)

Other: Spouse's benefits are gender neutral. You may be entitled whether you are the wife or the husband of the covered worker.

Note: The benefits may be suspended for any month that you do not have a child in your care. (see Sec. 207.8, CHILD IN CARE and Sec. 1008, SUSPENSION OF BENEFITS.)

❒ Section 204.3 Spouse's Benefits: Divorced Spouse

Other Names: Divorced Wife; Divorced Husband

Beneficiary Identification Code: B6 (*see* Sec. 1407.)

Requirements:

1. Your ex-spouse (the worker) is entitled to retirement or disability benefits.

NOTE: *Beginning January 1985, a divorced spouse may be* independently entitled *if divorced at least two years. This means the divorced spouse may receive benefits even if the worker has not yet filed or if his benefits are being suspended because of excess earnings.*

The two year requirement is designed to avoid any incentive for divorce solely to take advantage of this provision. If the ex-spouse has not filed, he must be "eligible"; he must be "insured" (see Chapter 6) and age sixty-two, or disabled;

2. you are the wife or husband of the worker as defined by SSA (see Sec. 207.5);

3. you had been married to the worker for at least ten years immediately before the divorce became final (you cannot add up the years married to one man if you were divorced and then re-married to the same man);

4. you file an application (see Chapter 4);

5. you are age sixty-two throughout the month (see Sec. 207.4). You cannot be entitled as a divorced wife if you are under age sixty-two even if you do have a child in your care;

6. you are not entitled to a higher retirement or disability benefit on your own account (see Sec. 302); and

7. you are unmarried.

Benefit Amount : same as aged spouse (see Sec. 204.1), but not subject to the Family Maximum

Termination: Entitlement ends with:

1. the same conditions for an aged wife (see Sec. 204.1); or

2. when you re-marry. However, you may continue to be eligible if you re-marry certain other Social Security beneficiaries. (see Sec. 904.)

❒ Section 204.4 Spouse's Benefits: Widow, Age Sixty and Over

Other Names: Widow's Insurance Benefit; Widower's Insurance Benefit; Aged Widow; Aged Widower

Beneficiary Identification Code: D (see Sec. 1407.)

Requirements:

1. The worker to whom you were married died fully insured (see Chapter 6);

2. you were "married" (see Sec. 207.5, THE MARRIAGE REQUIREMENT) to the worker;

3. you were married for at least nine months before the worker died (See Sec. 207.7 for exceptions to this requirement.);

4. you file an application (See Chapter 4, especially Sec. 405, for automatic conversion from wife to widow.);

5. you are at least age sixty;

6. you are not actually entitled to a higher retirement or disability benefit on your own account (see Sec. 303); and

7. you are not married (if you re-marry after age sixty then you are not married for Social Security purposes).

Benefit Amount: One hundred percent of the worker's Primary Insurance Amount (see Sec. 702) reduced for age, if you take it before Full Retirement Age, also subject to other reductions. (see Chapter 7.) See Chapter 3 if you also worked on your own account, especially Sec. 303.

Termination: Entitlement ends with:

1. the month before you become entitled to a higher retirement or disability benefit on your own account (see Sec. 303 for a discussion of dual entitlement);
2. if you are entitled based on a deemed marriage (see Sec. 207.5) benefits will end if another person becomes entitled as the legal widow or widower; or
3. the month before the month of death (see Sec. 1009).

Other: Widow's benefits are gender neutral.

☐ Section 204.5 Spouse's Benefits: Mother and Widow with Child Care

Other Names: Young Widow; Mother's Benefits; Father's Benefits

Beneficiary Identification Code: E (see Sec. 1407.)

Requirements:

1. The worker died fully or currently insured (see Chapter 6);
2. you were "married" to the worker (see Sec. 207.5);
3. you file an application (see Chapter 4, especially Sec. 405);
4. you are unmarried;
5. you are not entitled to a higher widow's benefits on another account or to a higher retirement or disability benefit on your own account (see Chapter 3, DUAL ENTITLEMENT); and

6. you have a "child in your care" (see Sec. 207.8).

Benefit Amount: Seventy percent of the worker's Primary Insurance Amount (Sec. 702) subject to the family maximum. (see Chapter 7.)

Termination: Entitlement ends with the month before the month in which any of the following occur (see Sec. 1009 for a general discussion of termination of benefits):

1. you become entitled to a higher benefit on another account;

2. the child in your care turns sixteen, unless the child is disabled and you are rendering services for that child (see Sec. 207.8, THE CHILD IN CARE REQUIREMENT). If you are entitled because you have a disabled adult child in your care, the benefits will end if the child is no longer disabled;

3. you re-marry (for exceptions if you re-marry another Social Security beneficiary, see Sec. 904);

4. if your entitlement is based on a deemed marriage (see Sec. 207.5), and another person becomes entitled on the account as the legal widow; or

5. the month before the month of death.

Other: If your benefits end because you have re-married, they may be reinstated if the subsequent marriage is terminated. (see Sec. 904.) Benefits are gender neutral.

❏ Section 204.6 Spouse's Benefits: Disabled Widow's Benefits; Age Fifty to Age Fifty-Nine

Other Names: Disabled Widow's Insurance Benefit, Disabled Widower's Insurance Benefit

Beneficiary Identification Code: W (see Sec. 1407.)

Requirements: the requirements are the same as for an aged widow (see Sec. 204.4), except that instead of being sixty you must meet the following requirements:

1. you are at least age fifty;

2. you are totally disabled (see Sec. 502);

3. the disability started not later than seven years after the worker's death or seven years after you were last entitled to mother's benefits (see Sec. 204.5) or disabled widow's benefits, if you were previously entitled; and

4. the disability lasts for more than five months (see Sec. 507) and is expected to last at least one year (see Sec. 502).

Benefit Amount: Seventy-one percent of the worker's Primary Insurance Amount. (see Sec. 702.) Before 1984, there was additional reduction for age for each month under age sixty. This is now eliminated. See Chapter 7 for a full discussion of computations of benefits.

Termination: Entitlement ends with the same events as the Widow (see Sec. 204.4), and when the disability ends. (see Sec. 513.)

NOTE: *For the Disabled Widow, re-marriage after age fifty is not considered for Social Security purposes, beginning in 1984.*

Other: Disabled Widow's benefits are gender neutral.

❑ Section 204.7 Spouse's Benefits: Divorced Widow's Benefits

Other Names: Surviving Divorced Wife; Surviving Divorced Husband; Divorced Widower; Divorced Mother; Divorced Father

Beneficiary Identification Code (Sec. 1407): D6 (divorced aged widow); E1 (divorced young widow—child in care); W6 (disabled divorced widow)

Requirements:

1. The worker died fully insured (for a young widow; currently insured (see Chapter 6));

2. you were legally married (note that the "deemed valid" marriage is not sufficient (see Sec. 207.5));

3. the marriage lasted for at least ten years immediately before the divorce;

4. you file an application (see Chapter 4);

5. you are age sixty, or disabled (see Sec. 502), or have a child of the worker in your care (see Sec. 207.8);

6. you are not entitled to a higher retirement or disabled benefit on your own account (see Sec. 303); and

7. you are unmarried.

Benefit Amount: Same as for a non-divorced widow, but not subject to the Family Maximum. (see Sec. 703.2.)

Termination: Entitlement ends under the same conditions described in Section 204.4 for an aged widow, Section 204.6 for a disabled widow, or Section 204.5 for a young widow.

CHILDREN'S BENEFITS

Section 205

☐ Section 205.1 Children's Benefits: Under Age Eighteen

Other Names: Surviving Child; Dependent Child

Beneficiary Identification Code: C (HC if the worker receives disability benefits) (*see Sec. 1407.*)

Requirements:

1. The worker is entitled to retirement or disability benefits, or, in the case of survivors, died either fully insured (see Sec. 602) or currently insured (see Sec. 603);

2. you are the child of the worker as defined in Sec. 207.9 below. Under certain circumstances this can include stepchildren, illegitimate children, adopted children, and grandchildren;

3. you are dependent on the worker at the time he becomes eligible for retirement or disability benefits or dies (see Sec. 207.10);

   NOTE: *If you are the natural child of the worker, you are deemed dependent.*

4. you file an application (see Chapter 4);

5. you are unmarried; and

6. you are under age eighteen. (See Sec. 205.2 for students and Sec. 205.3 for disabled adult children.)

Benefit Amount: Children entitled on a living worker's account receive fifty percent of the Primary Insurance Amount. (see Sec. 702.1.) Children entitled on a deceased worker's account receive seventy-five percent of the Primary Insurance Amount. In all cases it is subject to the family maximum. (See Chapter 7 for a full discussion of computations.)

Termination: Entitlement ends with the month before any of the following events occur (see Sec. 1009):

1. you turn eighteen (unless you are a student or disabled, see Secs. 205.2 and 205.3);

2. you marry;

3. the worker's entitlement ends for a reason other than death. If the worker dies, you will be converted to a survivor benefit as a child; or

4. you die.

☐ Section 205.2 Children's Benefits: High School Student

Requirements:

1. The requirements are the same as for a child under age eighteen, except that you do not have to be under age eighteen;

2. you must be no older than age nineteen. Benefits may continue for up to three months after age nineteen if you turn nineteen during the school quarter or semester;

3. you must be a full time student in an approved elementary or secondary school; and

4. you must not be paid by your employer to attend school.

Benefit Amount: Same as for a child under eighteen. (see Sec. 205.1.)

Termination: Same as for a child under eighteen (see Sec. 205.1); or if you are no longer a full time student; or if you start to be paid by your employer to attend school.

NOTE: *A school is considered approved if it is accredited by the state in which it is located and its primary purpose is to provide secondary or elementary education. Full time means twenty hours per week and at least a thirteen-week course.*

❏ Section 205.3 Children's Benefits: Disabled Adult Child

Other Names: Childhood Disability Beneficiary, Adult Disabled Child

Requirements:

1. The requirements are the same as Section 205.1, except that you must be age eighteen or older; and

2. you become totally disabled before you reach age twenty-two (Sec. 502).

   NOTE: *If your benefits stop when you turn age eighteen, they may be re-established if you become disabled before age twenty-two.*

Benefit Amount: same as for children under age eighteen. (see Sec. 205.1.)

Termination: Entitlement ends with:

1. under the same conditions described in Section 205.1 for children under age eighteen, except the age requirement. In some cases, marriage to another Social Security beneficiary does not terminate disabled child's benefits (see Sec. 1009);or

2. when the disability ceases. (see Sec. 513.) If you become disabled again after the disability ceases, the benefit may resume if you become disabled for the second time within seven years after the month in which your disabled child benefits ended.

❏ Section 205.4 Child's Benefits: Grandchildren

Other Names: These are referred to as Child's Benefits even though the entitlement is based on a grandchild relationship.

Requirements:

Grandchildren may be eligible for benefits if they meet the requirements for children's benefits discussed in the preceding sections and in addition meet these requirements:

1. You are the child of the covered worker's child (see Sec. 207.9);

2. your parents were both either deceased or totally disabled (see Sec. 502) at the time the grandparent first became entitled to retirement benefits, disability benefits, or died. If the grandparent died after becoming entitled to benefits, you must have met the requirements as of the date he or she became entitled to benefits; and

3. the grandchild is dependent on the grandparent. (see Sec. 207.10.)

Benefit Amount: The benefit amount of grandchildren's benefits is the same as for regular child's benefits.

Termination: The benefits end under the same conditions as for other types of child's benefits.

PARENT'S BENEFITS

Section 206

NOTE: *These benefits are payable only to surviving parents of deceased workers. They are not payable if the worker is alive.*

Beneficiary Identification Code: F (see Sec. 1407.)

Requirements:

1. The worker died fully insured (see Sec. 602);

2. you are the natural parent of the worker according to the laws of the state where the worker had a permanent home. If you adopted the worker, you must have adopted him or her before he or she was sixteen. If you are a stepparent you must have married the worker's natural parent before the worker became sixteen years old;

3. you are at least age sixty-two;

4. you have not married since the worker died;

5. you file an application (see Chapter 4);

6. you are not entitled to a retirement or disability greater than the parent's benefit amount; and

7. you received at least one half of your support from the worker at the time he died or became disabled if the disability continued up to the time of death.

   NOTE: *Proof of support must be filed with the Social Security Administration (SSA) within two years of the death of the worker or the date he became eligible for benefits. If this proof is not filed within two years of the worker's death or disability whether or not you are eligible to start receiving benefits at that time, you cannot be eligible at a later date, unless you can establish good cause for not filing it on time.*

   You may also be eligible for an exception provided by the Soldiers and Sailors Civil Relief Act of 1948. It would be wise to consult an attorney if the proof of support was not filed within two years of the worker's death or disability.

Benefit Amount: The amount of the parent's benefit depends on whether there are one or two parents entitled on the account. If there is one eligible parent, the benefit is eighty-two percent of the worker's Primary Insurance Amount. (Sec. 702.1.)

If there are two eligible parents, it is seventy-five percent of the worker's Primary Insurance Amount, payable to each parent. It is subject to reduction for the family maximum. (See Chapter 7 for a full discussion of computation of benefits.)

OTHER REQUIREMENTS

Section 207

❐ Section 207.1 Special Age Seventy-two Payments

Other Names: Prouty Benefits

In the 1960s, special legislation was passed to allow for special payments to very elderly people, even if they had not worked under Social Security or if they did not have enough work to qualify for regular benefits. There are only a handful of beneficiaries throughout the country who are eligible for these payments, almost all of whom are receiving them.

If you did not work at all, you must have attained age seventy-two before 1968 to be eligible. If you became seventy-two after 1967, you must have three quarters of coverage (see Sec. 605.1) for each year after 1966 and before the year you become seventy-two.

For men who became age seventy-two in 1972 or later, and for women who attain age seventy-two in 1970 or later, the work requirement for "fully insured" status (see Sec. 602) is the same.

We only mention these benefits in passing for the sake of being complete. These benefits are now almost completely phased out.

❏ Section 207.2 The Lump Sum Death Payment

A lump sum in the amount of $255 is payable to certain survivors of a worker who died fully or currently insured. (see Chapter 6.) A benefit is paid to only one person (with the exception of children, discussed below) according to the following order of priority:

1. the surviving spouse who was living in the same household with the worker at the time of death;

2. a surviving spouse not living in the same household but potentially entitled to monthly benefits on the deceased worker's account in the month of death; and

3. if there are neither of the above, then the payment is made to the surviving children of the worker who are eligible for monthly benefits on the account. All the surviving children split the lump sum death benefit evenly.

Only $255 is paid, even if it is split among the surviving children. If there are no people who fit these categories, there is no lump sum death benefit payable.

The application for this benefit must be filed within two years of the death of the worker.

❏ Section 207.3 Medicare

In this section we will discuss only the basic eligibility requirements for Medicare. Coverage provisions (what

Medicare pays for) are discussed in Chapter 12, and application requirements are discussed in Chapter 4.

Medicare has two parts: Hospital Insurance (Part A), and Medical Insurance (Part B). Hospital Insurance primarily pays for in-patient care, and Medical Insurance covers doctor bills. Both parts also cover other charges as well. (see Chapter 12.)

There are limits for filing an application for Medicare coverage. If you do not file in a timely fashion, you may lose coverage and have to pay an extra premium for Medical Insurance. (see Sec. 407.)

HOSPITAL INSURANCE

There are three groups of individuals eligible for Medicare Hospital Insurance. The first group are those age sixty-five or older who either:

a) receive any Social Security monthly benefit or Railroad Requirement Board monthly benefit, or are eligible for them. An application must be filed for Medicare even if you are still working (Sec. 404.3);

b) are federal employees with sufficient quarters of coverage (federal employees started having Medicare tax withheld from their paychecks effective January 1983). There are special provisions to grant credit for those employees for work performed before 1983, if they were employed by the Federal government in January 1984; or

c) pay a monthly premium and who are either U.S. citizens or lawfully admitted resident aliens who have resided in the United States for five continuous years or more.

The second group eligible for Hospital Insurance are those individuals who are entitled to monthly Social Security disability benefits (including disabled adult children and disabled widows) or disabled federal employees with enough work covered for Medicare purposes. The coverage for these groups begins with the twenty-fifth month of disability, not counting the waiting period. (see Sec. 507.)

The third group are those individuals who suffer from End Stage Renal Disease (kidney failure) and who undergo a regular course of dialysis or have a kidney transplant, and are either fully or currently insured (see Secs. 602 and 603); or are the spouse or former spouse (married at least ten years) of someone who is fully or currently insured; or, if under age twenty-five when kidney failure occurs, the child of a worker who is fully or currently insured.

NOTE: *The spouse or parent of the kidney patient need not be eligible for collecting Social Security benefits. For example, a wage earner who is age fifty and working full time is not eligible for monthly Social Security benefits, but his spouse, or children under twenty-five, can still be entitled to Medicare on his record under this provision.*

MEDICAL INSURANCE

There are three groups of people who are eligible for Medicare Medical Insurance.

The first group are those people age sixty-five or older who are U.S. citizens (or legal aliens admitted for permanent residence and who have resided in the country for five continuous years or more), who pay the monthly premium. You do not have to be eligible for Hospital Insurance or any other Social Security benefit to be eligible for medical insurance.

The second group of people are those eligible for Hospital Insurance on the basis of disability (see above), who pay the monthly premium.

The third group are those entitled to Medicare Hospital Insurance for the End Stage Renal Disease (see above), and who pay the monthly premium.

❒ Section. 207.4 Being Age Sixty-Two "Throughout the Month"

Social "Security" has a special rule that applies to retired workers and their wives who file for benefits beginning with age sixty-two. You can not receive a retirement benefit or an aged wife's benefit unless you are sixty-two throughout the entire month. Generally, this means that you cannot receive a Social Security benefit for the month of your sixty-second birthday, because you are not age sixty-two throughout that entire month. This rule does not apply to widows.

If your sixty-second birthday is on the first day of the month, you will be eligible because you will be age sixty-two throughout the month. If your birthday is on the second day of the month, then you will be eligible for that month as well, because for Social Security purposes you attain your age the day before your birthday.

In other words, if your birthday is August 2, you become age sixty-two on August 1 for Social Security purposes. Therefore you are eligible to receive the benefit for that month. If your birthday is on August 3, your first month of eligibility will be September.

Of course, you can be eligible for benefits for any month after the month you turn sixty-two.

☐ Section 207.5 The Marriage Requirement

In order to qualify for spouse's benefits or for widow(er)'s benefits, the claimant must have been married to the worker. Generally, this means that the marriage must be recognized as valid in the state where it was performed. A common law marriage will be accepted by Social Security only if entered into in a state which recognizes common law marriages. Most states do not.

A person may meet the marriage requirement even if he or she was not legally married to the worker, if the following conditions are met:

1. there was a marriage ceremony;

2. the claimant married the worker in good faith not knowing any impediment to the marriage;

3. the claimant was living with the worker at the time of his or her entitlement to benefits or at the time of death;

4. there is no other person entitled on the worker's earnings record as a legal wife or widow; and

5. the marriage is invalid because there was a legal impediment or there was a defect in the procedure followed in

connection with the marriage ceremony. A legal impediment exists, for example, where the worker was already
married at the time of this marriage.

This provision is called the *deemed valid marriage*. If your
benefits are based on a deemed valid marriage, they will end
if another person becomes entitled on the account as the
legal wife or widow. You may be re-entitled when that other
person's entitlement ends.

❑ Section 207.6 Exceptions to the One-Year Duration of Marriage Requirements for Spouse's Benefits

In most cases, to be eligible as the spouse of a worker, the marriage must have lasted for a least one year before eligibility
begins. However, there are some exceptions to this general
rule. These exceptions are as follows:

1. the claimant is the natural parent of the worker's child. This
   requirement is met if a live child was born to the worker
   and the claimant even though the child may not be alive at
   the time the claimant applies for benefits; or

2. the claimant was entitled or potentially entitled (under
   Social Security or Railroad Retirement) to spouse's benefits,
   widow's benefits, parent's benefits, or childhood disability
   benefits in the month before the month of marriage to the
   worker. *Potentially entitled* means that you could have
   received benefits if you had applied for them. Your age is
   not considered when determining whether or not you are
   potentially entitled.

❐ Section 207.7 Exceptions to the Nine-Month Duration of Marriage Requirement for Widow's Benefits

The general rule is that to be eligible for widow's benefits, you must have been married to the worker for at least nine months before the death of the worker. There are some exceptions to this rule. The exceptions which apply to spouses (see Sec. 207.6) also apply to widows, in addition to the following:

1. the worker died because of an accident;

2. the worker's death occurred in the line of duty while he or she was a member of a uniformed service on active duty; or

3. the claimant was previously married to the worker and divorced from him and the previous marriage lasted at least nine months.

NOTE: *For these three exceptions to apply, the worker must have been expected to live for at least nine months at the time of marriage.*

❐ Section 207.8 The "Child in Care" Requirement

If you are the wife or widow of a covered worker, you may be eligible for benefits at any age if you have a child of the worker in your care. To meet this requirement, the child must be entitled on the same earnings record as the one on which you are making your claim. The child must be under age sixteen or disabled. If the child is disabled and over sixteen, you can be eligible if you are performing personal services for the disabled child.

NOTE: *The child may continue to receive benefits until age eighteen, but your entitlement will end when the child turns sixteen unless he is disabled.*

The child does not have to be physically in your custody to meet the "in care" requirement. If you are exercising parental control and responsibility over the upbringing of the child, you may still satisfy the requirement. For instance, if the child is away at boarding school, you may still be eligible if you are reviewing his work and providing parental guidance.

NOTE: *If you are separated from the other parent of the child, you cannot meet the "child in care" requirement while the child is in the custody of the other parent. A child is considered in your care if he is with you at least one day of the month.*

If, for instance, the child goes to the other parent on July 15, and comes back to you on August 15, you will meet the requirement for both July and August. If the child did not come back until September 15, however, you will not meet the requirement for the month of August. For any month in which the child is not in your care, you are not entitled to benefits and they are suspended. Once the child returns to your care, the benefits may resume.

If the child is older than sixteen, but is disabled, you may still meet the "in care" requirement if you are performing personal services for the child. Personal services include such things as helping the child to bathe, feeding the child, dressing the child, and so forth. Personal services require that you render more services than for a non-disabled child.

❐ Section 207.9 The Child Relationship Requirement

In addition to natural children, certain other kinds of children can be eligible for Social Security benefits. These are adoptive children, stepchildren, equitably adopted children, and grandchildren.

To be eligible, an adopted child must have been adopted either before the worker became eligible for benefits or before the child became eighteen. If the child turned eighteen and was adopted after the worker became entitled, then the child must have received one-half support from the worker and lived with him for the twelve-month period preceding the worker's entitlement to benefits. The adoption must be legal.

The stepchild must be dependent on the worker (see Sec. 207.10) and the marriage of his parent to the worker must have lasted one year (nine months for survivor cases).

NOTE: *If the stepchild is living in the same household as the worker at the time of entitlement to benefits, the stepchild is deemed dependent. If the stepchild is entitled, the benefits will not be terminated even if the parents divorce at a later date.*

A child may be equitably adopted if there was an intent by the worker to adopt the child but he was unable to complete the legal requirements. If you have a possible case involving equitable adoption, you should consult an attorney.

Grandchildren may be eligible on the grandparents' account, but only if all of the requirements described in Sec. 205.4 above are met. Generally, this means that the parents are either deceased or totally disabled at the time the worker (the grandparent) becomes entitled to benefits, becomes disabled, or dies, whichever is earliest.

❏ Section 207.10 Dependency Requirements: Children and Grandchildren

The natural and adoptive children of a worker are deemed dependent on him. This means that there is no requirement for proof of dependency. A stepchild who is living with the worker at the time the worker becomes eligible does not have to prove dependency. However, in all other cases there must be proof that the child was dependent on the worker for at least one half of his support in the year before the worker became eligible for benefits, or died, in survivor cases.

Basically, Social Security will itemize all the reasonable and necessary expenses for the child's food, clothing, shelter and education, and will total these expenses. If the worker was making contributions to the child's support which were equal to or greater than half of these living expenses, the dependency requirement will be met.

ENTITLEMENT ON MORE THAN ONE ACCOUNT 3

IN GENERAL

Section 301

Under certain circumstances, you may be entitled to benefits based on two separate social security accounts. This chapter explains these situations.

NOTE: *Throughout this chapter, reference is made to unreduced benefits at age sixty-five. However, beginning with those born in 1938 for retirement and spouse benefits, and 1940 for widow's benefits, the age at which unreduced benefits are paid has increased. The increase of Full Retirement Age, as it is now called, will depend on the year of birth. See Section 703— "Reductions" for a full discussion. When the term "age sixty-five" is used in this chapter, it is meant to refer to Full Retirement Age.*

On Your Own Earnings Record and as a Wife

Section 302

If your Primary Insurance Amount (see Sec. 702.1) based on your own earnings record is less than half of your husband's you may be eligible for additional benefits on your spouse's account. If your husband is actually entitled to a retirement or disability benefit at the time you make your application for benefits (even if benefits are being suspended) you must file for spouse's benefits if your Primary Insurance Amount is less than one-half of your husband's.

Even if you intend to file only for spouse's benefits, if you have enough work credits on your own account you will be required by Social Security to file on your own account as well.

The general rules are that you must file on your own account if you have enough quarters of coverage to be fully insured (see Sec. 602), and that you must file on your spouse's account as a wife if your spouse is entitled to benefits and your Primary Insurance Amount is less than half of his.

This rule applies even if your husband is not actually receiving monthly benefits because they are being suspended (usually because of earnings). If he is not entitled because he has not yet applied, the rules do not operate because you cannot be eligible as a wife on an account that has not yet been established.

The rule that requires a wife to file on her husband's account even when his monthly benefits are being suspended can result in an unwanted reduction of the wife's benefit. This occurs when the husband is working, but is "entitled" to a retirement benefit that is not being paid because of the excess earnings. Even though no monthly benefit is being paid, he is legally entitled.

Let us say that the wife is age sixty-two and has worked on her own account. She applies for a retirement benefit, and her Primary Insurance Account is less than one-half of her husband's. She is required to file on his account as a wife. If she is not working (or is earning less than the allowable limit) she will receive a benefit on her own account reduced for age. (see Sec. 703.1.)

Assuming the husband's earnings are high enough that no wife's benefits are payable on the husband's account, the wife's benefit amount will be fixed at the full age reduction for age sixty-two. (see Sec. 703.1.) This means that if the husband stops working in two years when the wife is sixty-four, she will be paid the wife's benefit in addition to her own.

The amount of the wife's benefit will be reduced thirty-six months-which is the same as if she had been receiving it all along, instead of just twelve months (the amount it would be reduced if she were first entitled at exactly age sixty-four).

Fortunately, the reduction factor will be readjusted when she becomes sixty-five. (see Sec. 704.4.) However, for the twelve months for which she will receive the wife's benefit,before age sixty-five, she will suffer the full reduction.

A person who is entitled to a retirement or disability benefit and to a wife's benefit will receive the regular benefit on her own account, reduced for age if the retirement benefit is taken before sixty-five plus the difference between one half of the spouse's Primary Insurance Amount and her own. The difference will be reduced for age if taken before sixty-five, with the wife's reduction factor for age figured as of the time of entitlement to the wife's benefit.

Example: Howard and Wanda, who are husband and wife. They are both the same age; both have worked; and both are eligible for retirement benefits. Howard is working full time with substantial earnings.

Wanda is not working. They have just turned sixty-two. Wanda applies for her retirement benefit. Her Primary Insurance Amount is $500. Because she is sixty-two, the Primary Insurance Amount is reduced thirty-six months (for each month before age sixty-five) and the benefit amount is $400.

Two years later Howard retires and files for retirement benefits. His Primary Insurance Amount is $1200. Wanda decides to apply for wife's benefits on his account. (Note that she has the option of waiting until she is sixty-five to file for the wife's benefit.)

When she applied for her retirement benefit on her own account, her husband was not entitled to the benefits because he had not applied. Nevertheless, she applies for the wife's benefit now.

The amount is derived by taking one-half of her husband's Primary Insurance Amount ($1,200 divided by 2 = $600), subtracting her Primary Insurance Amount ($500) and then reducing the difference ($100) by the number of months she is before age sixty-five at that time, which is twelve.

Using the wife's reduction factor (Sec. 703.1), the $100 difference becomes reduced to $91. In this example then, Wanda receives $400 on her own account plus $91 on her husband's account.

ON YOUR OWN ACCOUNT AND TO WIDOW'S BENEFITS

Section 303

If you are potentially eligible on your own earnings record and on the record of your deceased husband (see Chapter 2 for ELIGIBILITY REQUIREMENTS), you have different options. You may receive benefits on your own account or on your husband's account.

If you are younger than age sixty-five, you may take reduced benefits on one account and switch to unreduced benefits on the other account at age sixty-five. We will discuss the rules that apply to these situations according to your age.

Under Age Sixty-two

If you are under age sixty-two you cannot receive retirement benefits on your own account. Beginning at age sixty you can receive regular widow's benefits. If you were born after 1928, the receipt of reduced widow's benefits will have no effect on retirement benefits on your own account if you switch later.

If you were born in 1928 or earlier, taking a widow's benefit before age sixty-two will cause a permanent reduction in your own retirement benefit. (see Sec. 703.1.) The dollar amount of reduction of the widow's benefit caused by entitlement to the widow's benefit before age sixty-two will be deducted from your retirement benefit even if you do not receive the retirement benefit until age sixty-five.

It will also be deducted from a retirement benefit payable before age sixty-five. However, if the regular age reduction for taking the retirement benefit before age sixty-five is greater, only the greater reduction is used, not both. Computation of benefit amounts is discussed fully in Chapter 8.

Example: Jane Doe reaches age sixty and applies for widow's benefits. Her husband's Primary Insurance Amount (Sec. 702.1) is $1000. The widow's age reduction factor (Sec. 703.1) causes a reduction of $285, bringing the monthly payment down to $715, based on sixty reduction months because Jane is sixty months under age sixty-five.

Jane has also worked and earned enough to be entitled to a retirement benefit on her own account. She continues to receive the widow's benefit until she turns sixty-five, and applies for benefits on her own account.

At sixty-five, she can receive an unreduced benefit on her own account, but the widow's benefit will stop. (If she was born before 1928, her own benefit would be reduced by $114 because she received widow's benefits for twenty-four months before she turned age sixty-two.) Of course, if the widow's reduced benefit is higher than her own benefit, she will continue to receive the widow's benefit amount.

Between Age Sixty-two and Age Sixty-five

At age sixty-two you can receive a retirement benefit on your own account or a widow's benefit on your husband's account. Whichever one you take, it will be reduced for age by the number of months you are under age sixty-five when you become eligible. See Section 703.1 for a discussion of reduction of benefits. You can take a reduced benefit on one account before age sixty-five, and then take the other one unreduced at age sixty-five (unless you were born before 1928 and have taken a widow's benefit before age sixty-two as discussed above).

Your decision as to which one to take now, and which one to take at sixty-five, can only be based on the dollar amount of each benefit, reduced and unreduced. Before making any decision, you must obtain benefit estimates. (see Sec. 1403.) When you contact Social Security make sure that you file a protective filing statement. (see Sec. 402.)

When you visit or call your local office, you should deal only with a Claims Representative. (see Sec. 105.) It is important to provide him or her with recent earnings information to obtain the most accurate estimates. (see Sec. 1403.) The ultimate decision can only be yours. Social Security cannot suggest which decision to make, they can only give you the information upon which to base it.

Example: Jane Doe retires at age sixty-two. She has worked under Social Security and is a widow. She goes to her District Office and learns that her Primary Insurance Amount is $1000 and that her deceased husband's Primary Insurance Amount is $1200. Her benefit reduced for age at sixty-two would be $800 (see Sec. 703.1), and her widow's benefit reduced for age at sixty-two would be $994. (see Sec. 703.1.)

She can receive either $800 on her own at sixty-two and $1,200 on her husband's at sixty-five, or $994 now on her husband's and $1,000 on her own at sixty-five. What should she do?

In the above example, no one can tell her what to do. She must consider her own particular circumstances, including her current income requirements. A helpful way to analyze the situation is this: Jane can receive an extra $194 per month for the thirty-six months she will receive benefits before age sixty-five if she takes the widow's benefit first, but she will get $200 less per month starting at age sixty-five, because the husband's unreduced amount is $1,200, as opposed to her unreduced amount of $1,000. If she does this she will receive a total of $6,984 more ($194 x 36 months) before age sixty-five.

If she does not take this higher benefit now, and instead decides to wait until sixty-five to get the extra $200 per month, it will take her thirty-five months after age sixty-five to get back the benefits she could have received before age sixty-five. This analysis does not take into account interest the extra money now could be earning, assuming it was invested.

Not counting interest, if Jane takes the widow's benefit at sixty-two instead of her own benefit, she will start losing money approximately three years after she turns sixty-five. If she takes the lower benefits on her own account at sixty-two, it will take her approximately three years after sixty-five to get back the money she passed up, but after that she will be ahead $200 per month.

If her income requirements allow, and if she expects a normal life span, it may very well be to Jane's advantage to take the lower benefit on her own account at sixty-two, and the higher widow's benefit at sixty-five. Of course, if she is on a tight budget, or does not expect to live past sixty-eight, she might be better off taking the higher benefit now.

Age Sixty-five and Older

If you are age sixty-five or older at the time you first become eligible for benefits, you will receive benefits on the account which has the higher benefit amount. See Chapter 7 for a complete discussion of the computation of benefit amounts.

As a Wife and as a Widow

Section 304

If you are a widow and have remarried, you may be eligible either as a widow or as a wife. Generally, widows who remarry cannot collect widow's benefits on their deceased husbands' records, unless they remarry at age sixty or older (age fifty for disabled widows, see Sec. 904). If you remarry after you turn sixty and your husband is eligible for retirement or disability benefits, you can receive benefits on whichever account gives you the higher benefit. Usually this reduction for age is only half of the husband's Primary Insurance Amount. (see Sec. 702.1.)

But in cases where the widow's benefit is less than the wife's benefit, you will receive the higher wife's benefit. Your entitlement as a widow, if you were receiving widow's benefits before you remarried or before your husband became eligible, will terminate upon your entitlement as a wife.

Since January 1984, divorced widows who remarry after age sixty (age fifty for disabled divorced widows) may continue to be eligible for the widow's benefits the same as non-divorced widows.

As a Wife and as an Ex-Wife
Section 305

If you are divorced from a person receiving Retirement or Disability benefits, you cannot receive benefits as an ex-wife if you have remarried. In these cases you can only receive benefits as the wife of your present husband if he is eligible for Retirement or Disability benefits. You must be married to your new husband for at least one year before you can be eligible, unless you meet one of the exceptions listed in Section 207.6.

As the Widow of Two or More Workers
Section 306

If you are the widow of two or more workers, you can receive benefits on the account which will give you the highest benefit. You cannot take one reduced widow's benefit under age sixty-five and then switch to another widow's benefit unre-duced at age sixty-five. Once you have picked which account to take benefits on, you cannot later change to a different husband's account.

DISABILITY BENEFITS AND RETIREMENT BENEFITS

Section 307

When a person age sixty-two to sixty-four is entitled to Retirement benefits and is also eligible for Disability benefits, he or she has the choice of taking one or the other of these. If you are age sixty-five or older, you can take only the Retirement benefit. This is equal to the Disability benefit. But if you are younger than sixty-five, the Retirement benefit is reduced for age. (see Sec. 703.1.)

The Disability benefit is not reduced for age, and so it is usually to your advantage to take the Disability benefit. However, if you have two or more eligible dependents, Retirement benefits may be better because the Retirement Family Maximum may be higher than the Disability Family Maximum. (see Sec. 703.2.)

There is a waiting period during which no Disability benefits are payable. This period is the first five full months of total dis-ability. (see Sec. 507.) If you are age sixty-two or older during one or more of the months of the disability waiting period, you can receive the reduced Retirement benefit during that time. The Retirement benefit will be reduced in the normal fashion depending on your age. (see Sec. 703.1.)

When your disability waiting period is over, you will then switch over to the Disability benefit. The Disability benefit will be permanently reduced, but only by the number of months you received Retirement benefits before switching to Disability, not by the full amount of the reduction used to figure the Retirement benefit.

If you die during the waiting period, widow's benefits will be permanently reduced by the amount of the retirement age reduction.

Example: John Doe becomes totally disabled beginning the month he becomes sixty-two. No Disability benefits are payable for the first five months, so he takes reduced Retirement benefits starting at age sixty-two. His Retirement benefit is reduced by thirty-six months, because he is thirty-six months under age sixty-five.

When his disability waiting period is up he switches over to Disability benefits. Because he received Retirement benefits for only five months before becoming entitled to Disability benefits, his Disability benefit is reduced by only five months.

CHILD ENTITLED ON MORE THAN ONE ACCOUNT

Section 308

A child under age eighteen or disabled before age twenty-two (see Secs. 205.1-205.4) may be entitled on more than one parent's, step-parent's or grandparent's account. In this case he will be paid on the account which gives the highest benefit.

As discussed in Section 703.2, when two or more dependents are entitled on one account, the Family Maximum can limit the total amount of benefits payable so that each dependent may suffer a reduction of the benefit amount payable to him.

However, when a child is entitled on more than one account, and there are other children entitled on one or more of these accounts, the Family Maximum for each account can be combined so that the reduction of benefits that would otherwise apply can be avoided, and each child can receive the full amount payable.

OTHER COMBINATIONS OF BENEFITS

Section 309

When a beneficiary is entitled to a combination of different benefits other than those discussed in the foregoing sections, the basic rule is that he or she will receive on the benefit that gives the highest monthly amount. If the beneficiary has worked long enough under Social Security to be entitled to a benefit on his or her own account, then a benefit on that account will be paid, even if it is lower. However, the difference will be added from the other account.

APPLICATIONS 4

In General

Section 401

NOTE: *The Full Retirement Age, i.e. the age at which one may receive an unreduced retirement, spouse or widow's benefit has been increased effective with those born in 1938 or later (1940 for widows), on a gradually increasing basis. (See Section 703 "Reductions" in Chapter 7 for a full discussion.)*

When we speak of unreduced benefits at age sixty-five in this chapter, we refer to Full Retirement Age, which varies depending on the year of birth. The charts in Section 703 show the Full Retirement Age based on the year of birth.

To be eligible for Social Security monthly benefits or Medicare, an application must be filed with the Social Security Administration (SSA). SSA has its own forms for applying for the different kinds of benefits, and these must be used.

It is a policy of most SSA offices not to mail out blank application forms, although sometimes they will mail out a blank application form to an attorney. They prefer for their own personnel to complete the applications. This does not necessarily mean that you have to make a personal visit to a District Office to file an application.

Telephone service is available for filing claims. (see Sec. 103.) To use this service, you will have to give all of your information over the phone to a Social Security employee, who will fill out the application and mail it out to you for your review and signature.

The date an application is filed can be very important. It can affect how much you can receive in past-due benefits. You can protect your filing date without having to file an application by filing a "protective filing statement." (see Sec. 402.)

Generally, if you believe that you are entitled to benefits, you should file an application. This will require SSA to make a formal decision on your claim. Also, it will protect your rights to any other benefits to which you may be entitled, and it will give you the right to appeal if you are dissatisfied.

Occasionally, a person is told that he cannot file an application because he does not meet some requirement. This is not true—you can always file an application. If you do not meet the requirements, the application may be denied, but that does not mean that you cannot file it. If there is any doubt, you should file the application to get a formal decision.

THE PROTECTIVE FILING STATEMENT

Section 402

Any written statement filed with SSA showing an intent to claim benefits can protect the filing date for an applicant who later files the formal application. In certain cases, this could be very important to prevent a loss of benefits that would otherwise be payable.

As discussed below in Section 406.1, an application for Retirement benefits may not be retroactive in certain cases. This means that you cannot receive benefits for any month before the month you filed the application, even if you were eligible. If a protective filing statement were filed, it would protect the filing date of an application filed at a later date to allow for the payment of back due benefits.

Example: John Smith turns sixty-two in January but is still working. He files a protective filing statement with his local District Office in January. In March, he is laid off and will have earnings less than the annual earnings limitation (see Sec. 802.1) so that benefits can be payable starting in January.

If he goes to his local District Office in April and files an application for retirement benefits, he can receive past due benefits starting with January, the first month he is sixty-two because he has filed a protective filing statement in January.

Let us take the same case except that John Smith *does not file* a protective filing statement with his local District Office in January. He goes to the Social Security office in April and files an application for benefits. He can receive benefits only starting in April. He will lose the benefits for the months of January, February, and March. A full discussion of the retroactivity rules for retirement cases is discussed in Section 406.1.

In order to qualify as a protective filing statement, the statement must be written, it must indicate an intent to claim benefits, and it must be signed by the claimant, by the claimant's spouse, or by a person who is qualified to sign an application. (see Sec. 403.) The protective filing statement must be filed with SSA and will protect benefits starting with the month in which it is filed.

SSA considers the protective filing statement filed as of the date it receives it or the date it is mailed by the U.S. Postal Service. In that case, the postmark will be used as the date of filing if that date is earlier than the date it is received by Social Security. Of course, it is a good idea to mail a protective filing statement by certified or registered mail, return receipt requested, so that you can prove the date it was mailed.

SSA will also accept the date a protective filing statement is filed with a Medicare-participating hospital of which you are a patient as a date of filing, as long as the hospital sends the statement to SSA.

After receiving a protective filing statement, SSA will send a notice to the claimant advising him that an application must be filed within six months. The protective filing statement will be effective for that six-month period. The six-month period

●

does not begin, however, until Social Security actually sends the notice. If they never do, then the protective filing statement can be good forever.

If you are eligible to receive benefits and you visit your Social Security office to obtain information about these benefits, you should file a protective filing statement even if you do not intend to claim benefits immediately. If it turns out a few months later that you could have been eligible when you visited the Social Security office, the protective filing statement could mean that additional benefits are payable to you.

When filing a protective filing statement, it is a good idea to get a copy. If you visit your District Office and the Claims Representative prepares a written statement for you to sign to protect your filing, ask the Claims Representative for a copy and also ask the him or her to date-stamp your copy so that you can prove that it was filed on that date.

Protective filing statements have been known to get lost in the local District Office. As long as you have your copy with a date stamp you will not have to worry about that. Likewise, when mailing a protective filing statement, you should send it by certified or registered mail to prove the date it was mailed, and you should also keep a copy of it.

There is no set format for the protective filing statement, but it should contain language similar to the following: "I wish to claim Social Security benefits." The statement should then be signed by the claimant, by the claimant's spouse, or by a person who would be qualified to file an application. (see Sec. 403.)

WHO MAY FILE AN APPLICATION

Section 403

The person who claims benefits must sign an application if he or she is eighteen years old or more, mentally competent, and physically able to sign. An application for child's benefits may be signed by a parent or a person standing in the place of a parent. A child between the ages of sixteen and eighteen may sign his or her own application if he or she is mentally competent, has no court appointed representative, and is not in the care of any person.

If the claimant is a minor, mentally incompetent, or physically unable to sign, an application may be signed by a court appointed representative or a person who is responsible for the care of the claimant, including a relative.

If the claimant is in the care of an institution, the manager of the institution may sign the application. SSA has the discretion to accept an application signed by someone other than a claimant if it is necessary to protect the claimant from losing benefits.

Example: Mr. Jones becomes bedridden at the end of a month due to a severe medical condition. He asks a neighbor, Mr. Smith, to go to the Social Security office to file an application for him before the end of the month so that he may receive the benefits for that month.

SSA may accept an application signed by Mr. Smith. However, it would be a good idea for Mr. Jones to sign a written statement saying, "I wish to claim Social Security benefits," and to give that statement to Mr. Smith to take to the Social Security office.

●

> There will be no doubt that such a statement is a protective filing statement and can protect that month's benefits. (see Sec. 402.)

Although persons other than the claimant may file an application under certain conditions, the claimant must be alive when the application is filed in order for it to be effective. There are some exceptions to this general rule.

One, if a disabled person dies before filing an application for disability benefits, a person who would be eligible to receive benefits due to a deceased beneficiary (see Sec. 1408) may file the application.

Although an application for disability benefits may be filed after the worker dies, such an application must be filed within three months after the month of death.

Example: John Smith dies in June of 1995. He was totally disabled for two years before his death, but never filed for Social Security benefits. He was married and his wife was living with him. She may file an application for the past due disability benefits as long as she makes the application or files a protective filing statement no later than September, the third month after his death.

The second exception to the rule is if a protective filing statement (see Sec. 402) was filed by the claimant and he died before an application was filed. In such a case, the date of filing is established by the date of the protective filing statement submitted by the claimant. An application may be filed by a person who would be eligible to receive benefits on the deceased's earnings record or by a person acting for the deceased's estate.

WHEN TO FILE AN APPLICATION

Section 404

❏ Section 404.1 In General

An application may be filed before the first month of entitlement. It will be effective until acted upon but no benefits will be payable until the first actual month of eligibility.

As noted in Section 406.1 through 407, there are different retroactivity rules for different kinds of applications. If an application is filed after the first month in which you are eligible for benefits, the application may or may not have the retroactive effect to entitle you to past due benefits. The application should be filed before the retroactive life of the application expires so that you do not lose benefits.

For example, in the case of a person who is older than sixty-five, an application can be retroactive for up to six months. (see Sec. 406.1.) If you turn sixty-five in March and have no earnings for March or later, you will be eligible for benefits.

In order to receive the maximum benefits, you must file the application no later than September. If the application is not filed until October, it can go retroactive for only six months so that benefits cannot begin before April and you will lose the month's benefits for March.

As noted in Section 407, it may be important to file an application before the month you turn sixty-five even if you do not intend to collect monthly benefits, to avoid losing some Medicare coverage.

❐ Section 404.2 When to File for Retirement Benefits

The rule of thumb frequently used is that you should file an application for Retirement Benefits three months before you plan to retire. This is good general advice.

However, there are certain situations in which you can actually lose benefits by following this guideline. The earnings test (see Sec. 801) and retroactivity rules (see Sec. 406.1) work together in such a way that hundreds or even thousands of dollars may be payable to you even though you are still working.

Depending on the amount of your annual earnings, and depending on the amount of your benefit, it is possible to receive some benefits even if you have not retired. An application (or a protective filing statement, see Sec. 402) must be filed at the right time, otherwise these benefits may be lost.

Example: John Smith will attain Full Retirement Age in December 2001; will work throughout the whole year of 2001; and will earn total annual earnings of $53,479. He goes to the Social Security office to file his application for Medicare coverage in September 2001. He learns that his unreduced benefit will be $1,000.

The benefit figured for January 2001 (an eleven month reduction for age—see Sec. 703.1) will be $938. Based on his annual earnings, the sum of

$9493 will have to be withheld from any benefits payable to him in 2001. (see Sec. 802.2.) If his month of entitlement to benefits begins with January 2001, a total amount of $11,256 ($938 x 12) would otherwise be payable for 2001. Only the amount of $9493 will have to be withheld based on his annual earnings, however, leaving the sum of $1763 payable for 2001.

However, because he did not file his application until September, he can go retroactive for only six months to March 2001. (see Sec. 406.1.) Only benefits for the months of March through December will be payable. Total benefits for these months (10 x $950 = $9500) are only $7 more than the amount that has to be withheld based on his annual earnings.

If he files his application in July or earlier in 2001, he will be eligible for the payment of $1,763 for 2001. Although the benefit is reduced for figuring benefits for January through November starting with the month he turns sixty-five it will be readjusted (see Sec. 704.4) and he will receive the full unreduced benefit thereafter.

When the readjustment occurs an additional $62 will be paid for December to bring the payment up to the unreduced amount (he turns sixty-five in that month). All future benefits will be unreduced.

Another situation in which benefits may be lost even though you file three months before you retire is if your yearly earnings will be less than the annual earnings limitations. (see Sec. 801.)

Example: Let us say that Jane Smith will reach Full Retirement Age in May 2002, at which time she plans to retire. Her yearly earnings will be less than $30,000, the yearly limit for those turning sixty-five in 2002.

She goes to her local Social Security office in February, three months before she reaches Full Retirement Age, and files an application for retirement benefits. She will be entitled to monthly benefits beginning with the month of February, the month she filed her application.

Because her annual earnings will be less than the annual earnings limitation, she is potentially eligible for benefits for all months of 2002. However, because payment of the benefit for the month of January would result in a permanent reduction for age, her application cannot be retroactive. (see Sec. 406.1.)

If she had filed her application in January, she would have been able to receive a benefit for that month. Although this would cause an extra reduction because of age, the reduction would be only a few dollars per month. She would receive hundreds of dollars for the January benefit.

It is impossible to know whether or not you should file an application for benefits before the usual three-month rule of thumb without knowing the exact benefit amount and the exact amount of your yearly earnings. However, if you will earn less than the annual earnings limit (see Sec. 801) in any year during which you are at least age sixty-two, you should file a protective filing statement (see Sec. 402) during the month of January of that year.

At the same time, you can request a benefit estimate (see Sec. 1403) and then make an informed decision as to when you should start your retirement benefits. (see Sec. 408.)

If you will be working during the year you turn sixty-five and earning over the applicable earnings limitation for the year, it would be a good idea to file a protective filing statement in January. You should do so no later than July of the year, and at the same time, you should obtain a benefit estimate.

In this way, if it turns out that you can receive benefits by having a January Month of Election (see Sec. 408), you will be protected. In 2002, if you turn sixty-five and have the maximum benefit, you can earn more than $85,000 and still receive some benefits for the year. If your spouse is also eligible on your account, some benefits may be payable even if you earn more than $115,000.

Of course, this all depends on your exact benefit amount and your exact yearly earnings. But to maximize the benefits payable for a year you are working, you should have a January Month of Election. You cannot have this if you do not file an application or protective filing statement before the end of July. A retirement application cannot be retroactive more than six months. (see Sec. 406.1.)

If you will have a "non-service" month (see Sec. 804) at any time after age sixty-two, you should file a protective filing statement no later than the first such month. This is a month in which your wages are below the monthly limit, and you do not perform substantial services in self-employment.

You may be eligible for a benefit for such a month, despite your annual earnings. In some cases you may not wish to take this benefit (see Sec. 408), but if you file the protective filing statement, you will preserve your option.

❐ Section 404.3 When to File for Medicare

Medicare has two parts: Hospital Insurance and Medical Insurance. (see Secs. 1202 and 1203.) An application for Hospital Insurance may be retroactive for six months.

However, unless you will be covered under your employer's group health plan, you must file for Medical Insurance before the month you turn sixty-five (see Sec. 407) to avoid losing some coverage.
Therefore, you should file for Medicare at least one month before you turn sixty-five, even if you are still working.

You now have the option of filing only for Medicare, without having to file for Retirement Benefits. Social Security prefers for you to file the retirement application even if you are working, and to place your benefits in suspense. Usually this makes no difference, but in some cases it does.

If you have a wife under sixty-five who will be eligible for benefits on her own account and yours, she may be better off if you file only the Medicare application, if you cannot receive benefits. If her benefit is less than half of yours, she will be required to file for spouse's benefits when she files for her own benefits if you are "entitled" on your retirement account, even if you are in work suspense.

If she is under sixty-five, this will cause the amount of her spouse's benefit to be reduced based on her age at that time. If you retire before she turns sixty-five, the extra age reduction for her spouse's benefit stays in effect until she turns sixty-five. (see Sec. 302.)

If you are self-employed, you may be able to exclude some of your income from earnings for purposes of the earnings limitation, but you may require a different month of entitlement for retirement. (see Sec. 408.)

If you have a "non-service" month (see Sec. 804) in the year you turn sixty-five, but do not wish to use it because you will have more non-service months in a later year, you may have to restrict your filing for Medicare only. (see Sec. 408.)

Social Security does not usually suggest that you split your entitlement to Medicare from retirement entitlement. It is up to you to specifically request this if it is to your advantage.

❐ Section 404.4 When to File for Survivor Benefits

As noted in Chapter 2, certain widows, widowers, children, and parents of deceased workers may be eligible for monthly benefits. The earliest such an application could be filed, of course, would be the month of death of the covered worker.

In the case of Child's Benefits, Mothers' or Fathers' Benefits (these are benefits payable to widows or widowers who have children under sixteen or disabled adult children in their care), and Parents' Benefits, there is no reduction for age. Therefore, an application for these types of benefits may be retroactive for up to six months. (see Sec. 406.1.)

Applications for these types of benefits usually should be filed within six months of the date of death. Of course, an application can be filed at a later date so long as the eligibility requirements are still met, but such an application can be retroactive for only six months and benefits may be lost if it is filed later than six months after the death. Sometimes, however, you may wish to start entitlement at a later date. (see Sec. 408.)

In the case of a disabled widow or widower between the ages of fifty and fifty-nine, an application can be retroactive for up to twelve months. (Sec. 406.1.) If you became disabled after your husband or wife died, you must file an application no later than seventeen months after the beginning of your disability to avoid a loss of any benefits. This is because there is a five-month waiting period before any benefits are payable. (see Sec. 507.)

If you became disabled before your husband or wife died, then you must file an application within twelve months of the month of death in order to avoid the loss of any possible monthly benefits. This is because the waiting period during which no benefits are payable may be used up during months before the death of your husband or wife.

In the case of benefits payable to widows or widowers age sixty and older, an application cannot be retroactive if it will result in a payment of a full monthly benefit reduced for age. (see Sec. 406.1.)

This means that if you file an application for widow's benefits before you are sixty-five, you cannot receive full benefits for any month before the month of filing. (The only exception to this rule is the widow who files for benefits the month after her husband dies. Her application can be retroactive one month to the month of death.)

Depending on the amount of your earnings and the amount of the benefit, some benefits may be payable even though you are working. (see Sec. 408.) Therefore, it is a good idea to at least file a protective filing statement (see Sec. 402) in the first month in which you may be eligible for widow's or widower's benefits, and then to obtain benefit estimates (see Sec. 1403) to determine whether or not you should file an application.

The same principles noted in Section 408 also apply to widow's claim. You may lose benefits in certain cases if you wait to file until three months before you plan to retire.

If you have worked on your own account and may be eligible for a Retirement Benefit in addition to the Widow's Benefit, you will have an option as to which one to receive. (see Sec. 303.)

If you are a widow but were entitled to wife's benefits before your husband died, you may not have to file an application. (see Sec. 405.)

❏ Section 404.5 When to File for Spouse's and Child Benefits

Generally, you should file an application for these types of benefits at the same time as the worker files. Child's Benefits (see Secs. 205.1-205.4) and Young Wife's Benefits (see Sec. 204.2) are not reduced for age, so usually there is no disadvantage to early filing. These applications may be retroactive for up to six months if the worker is retired. (see Sec. 406.2.) Applications filed after these periods may result in a loss of benefits.

As noted in Section 405, a worker should file a protective filing statement (see Sec. 402) in January of the year he turns sixty-five, even if he is working. If a wife may be eligible on the account, she, too, should file this statement.

If a person who may be eligible as a spouse files on her own record, she will be required to file as a wife as well, even if no wife's benefits are payable because of the husband's earnings. (see Sec. 302.)

See Section 408 for a discussion of some advantages to starting benefits at a date later than the first possible month of entitlement.

❑ Section 404.6 When to File for Disability Benefits

An application for disability benefits may be filed any time after a worker stops doing Substantial Gainful Activity. (see Sec. 504.) Basically, this means that you cannot file for disability benefits until you stop working. There is a full five-month waiting period before any disability benefits are payable. (Sec. 507.) You may file your application before this waiting period is up, although no benefits will be paid to you until then.

NOTE: *For a period of disability to qualify under Social Security, it must be expected to last for twelve months. (see Sec. 502.)*

As noted in Section 406.2, an application for disability benefits may be retroactive for up to twelve months. To avoid the loss of any monthly benefits, an application for disability benefits should be filed no later than seventeen months after the beginning of disability.

The first five months of the disability constitute the waiting period. Because the disability application can be retroactive for twelve months, you will not lose any benefits if the disability application is filed within seventeen months after the disability begins.

If your disability has already ended, you may still apply for disability benefits so long as the application is filed within twelve months of the end of your disability. (see Sec. 508.)

However, if you fail to file a disability application because your physical condition limited your activities to such an extent that you could not complete and sign an application, or if you were mentally incompetent, you may file an application for disability within thirty-six months of the end of the period of disability and still receive some benefits.

WHEN YOU DO NOT HAVE TO FILE AN APPLICATION

Section 405

In certain cases in which you are already entitled to one kind of benefit and then become entitled to a different type of benefit, you will be automatically changed over to the new kind of benefit without having to file an application. This is called *automatic conversion* and it occurs in three basic cases. These are as follows:

- The first case occurs when you are entitled to Wife's Benefits and your husband dies. If the basis of your entitlement as a wife is that you have a child in your care (see Sec. 207.8), you do not have to file an application for Mother's Benefits. Mother's Benefits are payable to widows who have children in their care.

  If you are entitled to Wife's Benefits based on age, you will be converted to Widow's Benefits automatically if you are sixty-five or older at the time of death of your husband.

  If you are under sixty-five, without a child in your care, your benefit will be automatically converted to Widow's Benefits only if you are not entitled to a benefit on your own account. This is because the widow has the option of receiving on her own account or on her husband's. (see Sec. 303.)

- The second situation in which you can be automatically converted to a new kind of benefit occurs when you are receiving Disability Insurance Benefits and turn age sixty-five. You do not have to file a new application for Retirement Benefits.

There will be no change in your benefit amount. You will simply be converted over to the retirement rolls and taken off the disability rolls. The amount of your Retirement Benefit will be the same as the amount of your Disability Insurance Benefit.

● The third situation in which automatic conversion occurs is when a child is entitled to benefits as a dependent, and the worker dies. Then the child will be automatically converted to surviving Child's Benefits and the benefit amount will be increased accordingly.

RETROACTIVITY RULES

Section 406

❑ Section 406.1 Retroactivity and Retirement and Survivors

Applications for these benefits (including dependent) can not be more than six months retroactive, and sometimes they may have less, or no, retroactivity. *Retroactivity* means that you can be entitled to benefits for months before the month of filing. If you file a protective filing statement (see Sec. 402), your formal application is considered filed in the month the protective filing statement is filed, if that is an earlier month.

Retirement and survivor applications may not be entitled to the full six months retroactivity if the benefits payable before the month of filing are reduced for age. (see Sec. 703.1.) If they are not reduced for age, either because you are over sixty-five or because they are not subject to age reduction, then the application has a full six-month retroactivity.

Benefits reduced for age are Retirement (Sec. 202), Aged Wife's (Sec. 204.1), and Aged Widow's (Sec. 204.4) if they are paid before Full Retirement Age (Sec. 703).

Benefits not reduced for age are Young Wife's (Sec. 204.2), Mother's (Sec. 204.5), Child's (Sec. 205.1-205.4) and Parent's (Sec. 206).

Applications for Disabled Widow's Benefits (Sec. 204.6) may be retroactive for up to twelve months, the same as applications for regular Disability Benefits. (Sec. 406.2.)

Example: Harry turns sixty-five in January; his wife Wanda is age sixty-three. They both file their applications the July after Harry's sixty-fifth birthday. Neither Harry nor Wanda has earnings over the applicable limits. (see Sec. 801.)

Harry's benefits can begin with January because this is no more than six months before the month of filing. The retroactive benefits are not reduced for age because his is sixty-five.

Wanda's benefits cannot start before July, the month of filing, because the retroactive benefits are reduced for age since Wanda is sixty-three. (see Sec. 703.1.)

NOTE: *If she had filed a protective filing statement (see Sec. 402) in January, her benefits could begin as of January even though the application was not filed until July.*

Wives and Widows

Wife's Benefits are subject to withholding due to the worker's earnings. (see Sec. 803.) Even so, an application for Wife's Benefits cannot be retroactive if the applicant is under sixty-five, even if her husband's can be. Of course, if she is entitled as a wife because she has a child in her care (see Sec. 204.2), her application may be fully retroactive (six months) because this type of Wife's Benefit is not reduced for age.

Aged Widow's Benefits (see Sec. 204.4) are reduced for age if taken before age sixty-five. (see Sec. 703.1.) Therefore, applications may not be retroactive if benefits would be reduced for past months.

An exception is for the widow who files in the month after the month of the worker's death. The application may be retroactive for only one month. If the application is filed in the second or later month after the month of death, it may not be retroactive.

If the amount of the widow's benefit is already reduced due to the husband's receipt of reduced retirement benefits in his lifetime (see Section 703.1 regarding reductions for widow's benefits) then the application may be retroactive for up to six months even for a widow under age 65, so long as the first retroactive month of entitlement is subject to this benefit limitation.

❒ Section 406.2 Retroactivity and Disability

An application for Disability Insurance Benefits or Disabled Widow's Benefits can be retroactive for up to twelve months. This means that if you are otherwise eligible for disability benefits within the twelve months before the month in which you file your application, you may be paid for them. You may not be paid for months previous to the twelve month-period before the month in which you file your application.

For example, you become disabled on January 11, 2000. No benefits are paid for the first five full months of disability (see Sec. 507), so that for February through June, no benefits will be payable. (January does not count because it is not a *full* month of disability.) Beginning with July 2000, benefits can be payable.

Assume that you do not apply for disability until September 2001. Because the application can be retroactive for only twelve months, the first month for which you can receive disability benefits will be September 2000.

When your claim is approved, the first payment will include payment for September 2000 to date. You will lose the benefits for July 2000 and August 2000.

Applications for Child's or Wife's Benefits on the account of a wage earner who is entitled to Disability Insurance Benefits are also entitled to the twelve-month retroactivity, with the exception of Aged Wife's Benefits (see Sec. 204.1), if the wife is under sixty-five. In this case, the rules in Section 406.1 apply to her.

If you were disabled in the past but have recovered and returned to work, you may still apply for the disability benefits for the past months you were disabled (see Sec. 508), but only for those months within twelve months of the date you file your applications.

There is an exception to the twelve month retroactivity rule for applying for a *period of disability*. If you were mentally incompetent or your physical condition limited your activities so that you could not complete and sign an application, you may file for a period of disability within thirty-six months of the end of the disability. Although no benefits can be paid more than twelve months retroactively, if a period of disability is established, a "freeze" (see Sec. 503) can be placed on your earnings record.

RULES ON MEDICARE ENROLLMENT

Section 407

To be eligible for Medicare coverage, you must be sixty-five or have been disabled and receiving social security benefits (including Disabled Widow's and Disabled Adult Children) for twenty-four months. This is in addition to the full five-month waiting period.

In other words, at the time you receive your twenty-fifth Social Security disability check, you will be eligible for Medicare coverage. Medicare coverage is also available for those who are on kidney dialysis. (see Chapter 12.)

As noted in Chapter 12, Medicare has two parts: Hospital Insurance and Medical Insurance. These have been referred to in the past as Part A (Hospital Insurance) and Part B (Medical Insurance). Officially, Social Security no longer uses these letters to designate the different parts of Medicare because they can cause confusion with beneficiary identification codes. (see Sec. 1407.)

You may apply for Hospital Insurance at any time after you become eligible. An application for this part of Medicare coverage can be retroactive for no more than six months. If you are receiving monthly benefits when you first become eligible you will be enrolled automatically.

The rules are very different when it comes to Medical Insurance. This part of Medicare covers doctors bills. (see Sec. 1203.)

To be covered at the earliest time, you must apply for Medical Insurance *before* your first month of eligibility. Medical Insurance is optional. You must pay a premium for it even if you are entitled to regular monthly benefits.

If you are receiving benefits at the time you become eligible, you will be notified that Social Security will automatically enroll you in Medical Insurance and will start deducting the premiums from your benefit checks. If you are not entitled to monthly benefits at the time you turn sixty-five, you must apply for Medical Insurance yourself.

If you apply for Medical Insurance (also called *supplementary medical insurance*) *before* the month you turn sixty-five, coverage will begin on the first day of the month in which you turn sixty-five. If you apply for Medical Insurance *during* the month you turn sixty-five, it will become effective on the first day of the following month.

If you apply the *month after* you turn sixty-five, your coverage will begin on the *third month* after you reach sixty-five. Filing during the *second month* after sixty-five grants you coverage starting the *fifth month* after you are sixty-five. Filing in the *third month* covers you starting in the *sixth month* after your sixty-fifth birthday.

If you do not apply for Medical Insurance within three months after the month you turn sixty-five, then you are limited as to when you can apply for it and when it can begin. The period of time around your sixty-fifth birthday, including the month of your sixty-fifth birthday, the four months before your sixty-fifth birthday, and three months after your sixty-fifth birthday are referred to as the *Initial Enrollment Period*.

If you do not apply for Medical Insurance during this time, then you can only apply during the first calendar quarter of any year thereafter. This is the *General Enrollment Period*, consisting of January, February, and March of any following calendar year.

If you miss your Initial Enrollment Period and then apply for Medical Insurance during a General Enrollment Period, Medical Insurance coverage will not become effective until July 1 of that year. Additionally, if you have gone twelve months or more without having Medical Insurance coverage since your first month of eligibility, the premium that you must pay for Medical Insurance will be increased. (see Sec. 1203.)

If you have not enrolled in Part B (Medical Insurance) because you were covered by an employer group health plan (see Sec.

1204), you are entitled to a *Special Enrollment Period*. This is a seven-month period beginning with the first month that your group coverage ends. You may enroll in Part B during this time.

If you enroll in the first month, your Part B coverage begins with the first day of that month. You should do this to avoid a gap in coverage.

If you enroll in a later month of the Special Enrollment Period, your coverage begins with the first day of the *following* month.

If your group coverage ends before the end of a month, that month will be considered the first month of your Special Enrollment Period *if* you sign up for Part B during that same month. This way you will not have any gap in coverage. Otherwise, the first month will be the *next* month (the first full month in which you are not covered by the group plan).

You are also entitled to a Special Enrollment Period near the time you turn seventy, because your employer is not required to cover you after age seventy. This Special Enrollment Period begins with the third month before the month you turn seventy and lasts seven months.

If you enroll during one of the first three months, your Part B coverage begins with the month you turn seventy. If you enroll during the month you turn seventy or during a later month, coverage begins on the first day of the month *after* your month of enrollment.

To avoid any gap in coverage, you must enroll *before* the month you turn seventy.

NOTE: *Social Security considers you to turn seventy the day before your seventieth birthday. This is important if your birthday is on the first day of the month. If you lose group coverage during the month you turn seventy or earlier, the rules stated in the first two paragraphs of this section will apply if following them will give you coverage earlier.*

To be eligible for the Special Enrollment Period, you must be covered *both* by Hospital Insurance (Part A) *and* by the group plan in at least one month. If you are not already covered by Part A, you must apply for it. The application may be retroactive for no more than six months. For this reason, if you do not have Part A, you *must* file *before* the seventh month of the Special Enrollment Period.

You are limited to one Special Enrollment Period if you do not enroll in Part B when you first become eligible for it (i.e., during your Initial Enrollment Period). If you do enroll then, but later cancel, you may have more than one Special Enrollment Period only if you are covered by both Part A and a group plan when you cancel Part B. Additionally, you must enroll in Part B during a Special Enrollment Period each time you lose group coverage.

These rules also apply if you have group coverage based on your spouse's employment, regardless of your spouse's age.

Even if you do not plan to retire, you should contact your local Social Security Office before the month you turn sixty-five so that you can apply for Medicare without losing any coverage or having to pay any additional premiums.

WHEN TO START YOUR BENEFITS— THE MONTH OF ELECTION

Section 408

As noted in Sections 406.1 and 406.2 above, applications for monthly benefits may, in certain circumstances, be retroactive. This means that you may begin your legal entitlement in a month previous to the month you file your application. If you are filing for a type of benefit that is not reduced for age, such as Young Wife's Benefits (Sec. 204.2) or Mother's Benefits (Sec. 204.5), then there is no disadvantage to beginning your legal entitlement at the earliest possible time, with some exceptions discussed below. However, if you are applying for a benefit which may be reduced for age and you are under sixty-five, you may have to make a choice.

For example, Retirement Benefits and Widow's Benefits paid before sixty-five are reduced for age. (see Sec. 703.1.) As a result, if your entitlement to benefits begins earlier than the month you apply for benefits, it will be reduced by a larger amount because of the age reduction. You will be younger when the entitlement begins so that the benefit will be reduced more.

However, sometimes the additional benefits you gain by going retroactive as far as possible can offset the amount of the extra reduction. You may be better off starting your benefit at an earlier date. For Retirement or Widow's Benefits, the month you choose your legal entitlement to benefits to begin is called *The Month of Election.*

Example: John will reach Full Retirement Age in September 2001. He plans to work through the month of August 2001 and his total earnings for that year will be $40,480. He will retire in September 2001. He goes to his local District Office in June to fill out his application.

He is informed that his Primary Insurance Amount is $900. The Primary Insurance Amount is the unreduced benefit amount. Because John will be working and earning money through the month of August and he will reach Full Retirement Age in September, he assumes that his entitlement to benefits should begin in September. However, it will be to his disadvantage to start his benefits in September.

It works like this:

John's 2001 earnings will be $40,480. By applying the Work Test (see Sec. 802.2), we find that $5160 must be withheld from benefits payable for months in which John will earn over $2,083 (a full discussion of the Work Test is found in Chapter 8). This means that the months of January through August are subject to withholding of benefits.

If John's Month of Election is January, his $900 Primary Insurance Amount is reduced to a benefit amount of $859 per month because he is eight months under Full Retirement Age as of January. Applying the Work Test, we know that the sum of $5,160 must be withheld from benefits. But for the months of January through August, the total of benefits, at $859 per month, is $6,872. This leaves $1,712 in benefits payable for this period.

The monthly benefit of $859 will be withheld in full from January through June and the sum of $6 will be withheld from the July benefit, leaving $853 payable for July. The benefit amount of $859 for the month of August is payable so that John will receive total benefits of $1712 for July and August (a partial benefit of $853 for July and a full benefit of $859 for August).

If you are under sixty-five an application for Retirement Benefits can be retroactive for up to six months if benefits payable before the month of filing are charged against excess earnings. (see Sec. 406.1.) This is the case with John. The benefits payable for January through June and part of July's benefit are actually payable before the month he applies.

Therefore, he can start his legal entitlement to benefits with January. By doing so, he will use up the amount of benefits that will have to be withheld ($5,160) before he stops working. By doing this, he will be paid a benefit for the month of August and a partial benefit for the month of July in the total amount of $1,712.

John's benefit will be adjusted to take out any reduction for a month before sixty-five in which he did not receive a full monthly benefit. (see Sec. 704.4.) In John's case, he received a full monthly benefit before sixty-five only for the month of August. The month of July does not count because part of the benefit for that month was used to satisfy the Work Test.

Therefore, at sixty-five, the reduction months will change from eight reduction months, used to figure his benefits as of January to only one permanent reduction month for August. Because of this readjustment, as of September his benefit will be reduced by only one month so that the benefit amount will be $894. Although he suffers a permanent reduction in the amount of $6 per month, he has received $1,712 in benefits before sixty-five.

Instead, if John were to start his legal entitlement with the month of September, the month he turned sixty-five, he would receive no benefits for the period of January through August and would receive $900 per month starting with September.

Although he would get $6 more per month, he would not have the $1,712 that he would get with a January Month of Election. If John passed up the opportunity to get his additional $1,712 in benefits before sixty-five, it would take him twenty-three years to get that money back, without figuring interest!

Clearly it is to John's advantage to start his legal entitlement as of January instead of September even through it means a small permanent reduction in his monthly benefit.

NOTE: *John must file his application no later than July, because an application for Retirement Benefits cannot be more than six months retroactive in any event.*

Of course, if John were to file a Protective Filing Statement (see Sec. 402) before July, it would protect his filing date for this purpose.

These principles also apply to Widow's Benefits that may be reduced for age.

As a general rule, especially in the year you turn sixty-five, it is to your advantage to start your month of entitlement as early in the year as possible. Of course, it all depends on your

Primary Insurance Amount, your expected yearly earnings, and your age.

When deciding whether to start your legal entitlement with the earliest possible month or with a later month, you should consider how much in benefits you can receive before the later month, and how much extra reduction for age that will cause. You should also note that the adjustment of the reduction factor occurs at sixty-five.

Therefore, if you take an extra reduction for age, the monthly benefit amount will not be changed to eliminate months that are not payable until you turn sixty-five because of earnings. If you take a reduced benefit at age sixty-two, that reduced benefit amount will stay in effect until you turn sixty-five.

Sometimes you may be better off with a later month of entitlement. If you are self-employed, you should consider a special rule that excludes self-employment income from earnings for purposes of the retirement test. (see Sec. 808.) Self-employment income received after your first *year* of entitlement, but attributable to services rendered before the *month* of entitlement will not be included.

Example: Jim is a self-employed plumber who turns sixty-five in July 2001. He expects $50,000 net earnings in 2001, and $50,000 net earnings in 2002. $7,500 of his expected 2002 earnings will result from services rendered in 2001, but before December 2001.

When he files for Medicare, he learns that, based on his expected 2001 earnings and his benefit amount, he can receive $600 in benefits for 2001 with a

January 2001 month of election, without suffering any permanent reduction in his benefit.

However, because of the special exclusion rule, he will be better off with a December 2001 month of election, even though he loses the $600. With a December 2001 month of election he can exclude the $7,500 he expects to receive in 2002 from that year's countable earnings because it is attributable to services rendered before December 2001, his month of entitlement, and received after the first year of entitlement.

This means his 2002 countable earnings will be only $42,500. Under the one for three rule (see Sec. 801) he will receive $2,500 more in 2002 benefits than if his countable income were $50,000. When he files for Medicare in 2001, he will have to limit his application to Medicare only. (see Sec. 404.3.)

If your earnings are high enough to prevent payment of benefits, but you are eligible for a "non-service" month (Sec. 804), you may wish to forego this benefit if you will have more non-service months in a later year and wish to use them then. Generally you are eligible for non-service months in only one year.

Example: Bill is a merchant who earns $90,000 a year and does not plan to retire. However, in July 2000 he will not work and may be eligible for benefits for that month.

In 2001 he will have the same annual earnings, but will not work in February, July, or August. Clearly, he is better off if he receives benefits for three non-service months in 2001, rather than only one in 2000. To do this, his first month of entitlement must be later than July 2000. If he is eligible for Medicare earlier, he may restrict his filing for Medicare only. (see Sec. 404.3.)

At one time, you could not change the Month of Election that you chose when you filed your application unless you withdrew the application. Now, the Month of Election is conditional and can be changed at a later date so long as the new Month of Election is within the retroactive life of the application. (see Sec. 406.1.)

You will require the assistance of a Claims Representative to figure out your best Month of Election in close cases. When you visit your District Office to discuss this, make sure that you have as accurate an estimate of annual earnings as possible. Also, make sure that you file a Protective Filing Statement (Sec. 402) with your District Office no later than July (preferably in January) of the year in which you turn sixty-five so that you may take advantage of a January Month of Election if that would result in extra benefits.

If you go to your District Office to get a benefit estimate (see Sec. 1403) and to discuss this question, make sure that your last two years' earnings are included (bring your W-2 forms or tax returns) and that your estimated earnings are as accurate as possible.

For a complete discussion of the choices that a widow entitled to a Widow's Benefit, as well as a benefit on her own account, must make, see Section 303.

REQUIRED DOCUMENTS

Section 409

❐ Section 409.1 In General

You need different documents depending on what type of claim you file. These will be discussed in more detail in the following sections. Social Security always requires original documents. You cannot give them a photocopy of a birth certificate or W-2 form. It will not be accepted without the original.

Sometimes clerks in Vital Statistics Offices will give you a photocopied birth certificate. If this is the case, make sure that the photocopy has an original raised seal or is stamped and signed by the clerk. This is what is referred to as an original copy.

When you bring your documents into Social Security, they will make their own photocopies and return the documents to you. As noted above, however, you cannot give them the photocopies in the first instance; they must see the actual original documents.

Sometimes people delay filing a claim for benefits because they do not have all of their required documents together. This can be a very bad mistake, because it can result in the loss of benefits. Do not wait to gather all of your documents together before filing your claim. Although it is a good idea to have the documents on hand when you file, it is not a good idea to delay filing. You can file an application and submit the documents at a later time when you get them. Sometimes Social Security will get them for you.

It is important that your application be filed at the earliest possible time so that you may receive all the benefits to which you are entitled. If you are late in filing the application, you may lose benefits. Of course, it will speed the processing for you to have your documents together when you file your claim, but you should note that the processing of the claim can begin even without all the documents.

Try to get your documents together well before you intend to file your claim, but when it comes time to file do not delay even if you do not have them all.

❏ Section 409.2 Required Documents for Filing a Retirement Claim

When you file a claim for Retirement Benefits, you need your birth certificate or other acceptable proof of age. (see Sec. 410.) You also need all W-2 forms for the last two years. The W-2 forms are the statements of earnings issued by each employer and show your total annual earnings.

The reason you need these documents is that Social Security's records of earnings are behind by at least one year and sometimes two. These W-2 forms establish your earnings so that they can be used to figure your benefit.

NOTE: *If you have had more than one employer, you should make sure you bring W-2s from each one. Also, some people* *receive W-2 forms from a union or some other source of earnings. Make sure you bring these as well.*

If you are self-employed, you will need the last two or three years' income tax returns for yourself as well as for your business. (see Sec. 412.)

❑ Section 409.3 Required Documents for Filing a Wife's Claim

When you file a wife's or husband's claim, whether because you are sixty-two or because you have children in your care, Social Security requires your birth certificate. However, a marriage certificate is not required. Instead, Social Security requires your husband or wife to sign a form that certifies that you are presently married.

NOTE: *If you are filing an application on your own earnings record as well, you should bring your last two years' W-2 forms if you have worked within the last two years. (see Sec. 409.2.)*

If you are filing as a divorced wife (see Sec. 204.3), you will need your marriage certificate and final divorce decree.

❑ Section 409.4 Required Documents for Filing a Widow's Claim

When you file a claim for Widow's Benefits, you will need your husband's death certificate, your own birth certificate, and your marriage certificate. If you file as a Surviving Divorced Wife, you also need your divorce papers. Additionally, if your husband had worked within the last two years, you need his W-2 forms from all of his employers.

NOTE: *If you were receiving Wife's Benefits you may not have to file a new application. (see Sec. 405.)*

❏ Section 409.5 Required Documents for Filing a Child's or Parent's Claim

When filing a child's claim, you need a birth certificate for each child. If the child is a stepchild, the marriage certificate of the natural parent to the worker is also required to establish the relationship. For adopted children, the adoption papers are required. For illegitimate children, it has to be proven that the father acknowledged the child as his own before becoming entitled to Social Security benefits or before dying.

The proof can take the form of a report card signed by the father or a signed hospital bill from the time of the birth of the child, or other such documents. Any written acknowledgment will suffice.

In the case of a person filing as a grandchild, there must be proof of death (a death certificate) or disability of both parents, as well as birth certificates of the grandchild and the parents to establish the relationship to the worker. Disability is not something you can get in a document. You must supply names and addresses of treating doctors and hospitals. Social Security will obtain the records.

❏ Section 409.6 Required Documents for Filing a Disability Claim

We do not discuss medical evidence or medical requirements in this section; we only discuss documents that must be produced at the time the application is filed. For a person who is filing for disability benefits on his or her own account, a birth certificate will be required if the person is born in 1930 or later, or if you are age fifty-nine and a half or older at the time the application is made.

Proof of age is required if you were born in 1930 or later because there is a special insured status requirement for persons who turn twenty-two after 1951. It is SSA's policy to obtain a birth certificate for persons who are fifty-nine and a half or older at the time of the application so that they can be changed over to the Retirement Benefits at age sixty-five without having to re-contact the beneficiary for proof at that time.

NOTE: *Social Security will not require you to submit any documents in connection with the disability claim until such time as your claim is allowed on the medical evidence.*

Most disability cases are denied. Therefore, Social Security does not go out of its way to get documents or to require you to get documents until the claim is allowed on medical grounds.

Of course, if you have the documents you should submit them when you file because if they are in the file, Social Security can pay you benefits as soon as the claim is allowed. Otherwise, they may have to contact you again after the claim is allowed to obtain the necessary documents.

PROOF OF AGE RULES

Section 410

Most Social Security beneficiaries receive benefits on the basis of their age. SSA has very precise guidelines and requirements for proof of age.

SSA classifies proof of age into two basic categories: Primary Evidence and Secondary Evidence. SSA considers Primary Evidence of age to be either a birth certificate or a baptismal certificate recorded before the age of five.

Usually a birth certificate or a baptismal certificate will contain not only the date of your birth, but will also show the date that the document was first recorded. Sometimes a birth certificate is not recorded until years after a person's birth.

If your birth or baptismal certificate was not recorded within five years of birth, it will not be accepted as Primary Evidence.

NOTE: *You do not need both a baptismal and a birth certificate; either one will do.*

If you do not happen to have a birth certificate or a baptismal certificate with you at the time you file your application, SSA will not accept other evidence of your age unless there is a satisfactory explanation of why there is no Primary Evidence.

If you were not baptized, obviously you cannot be expected to have a baptismal certificate. However, if you claim that there is no birth certificate for you, SSA may require a statement to that effect from the State Bureau of Vital Statistics.

Years ago, some states did not record births. SSA has a list of all of these states. If the state in which you were born did not record births at the time of your birth, that will be satisfactory evidence of the unavailability of a birth certificate.

However, if your state did record births at the time you were born, Generally, SSA will require some proof that there is no birth certificate. Such proof would be a statement from the

Bureau of Vital Statistics of your state that they searched for your birth certificate and could not find one.

If there is no Primary Evidence as discussed above, then SSA will consider what is referred to as *Secondary Evidence*. Secondary Evidence includes such things as a birth certificate or baptismal certificate recorded more than five years after birth, and passports, census records, marriage certificates that show your age, immigration records, and so forth. (See Appendix 1 for a listing of types of Secondary Evidence that Social Security will consider.)

Additionally, when you applied for your social security number you were asked to give your date of birth and Social Security still has that information.

If you submit one piece of Secondary Evidence, as listed in Section I-1 through I-9 of the list in Appendix 1, and it agrees with the date of birth you gave when you applied for a social security card, no further evidence will be required.

However, if you submit two or more pieces of evidence that contain different dates of birth or if there is any discrepancy between the date of birth you gave when you filed for your social security number and any Secondary Evidence, then SSA will require full development of Secondary Evidence.

In this event, they will attempt to get as much as possible of the evidence listed in Appendix 1. Then they can make a determination to establish your date of birth.

When considering the different kinds of Secondary Evidence, SSA will generally prefer evidence that is oldest and that is least likely to be subject to error.

For instance, a birth certificate recorded at age seven would be considered very good Secondary Evidence because it was recorded early in life and for a purpose that generally would require that exact date of birth.

Generally, date of birth on a marriage certificate or an employment record is not considered very good evidence because usually it is recorded later in life and the purpose for which it is recorded does not require the exact date of birth.

If there is a piece of evidence that shows your date of birth as being different, such as an employment record or your date of birth on the social security number, you will be asked to explain this difference. Many people gave a different date of birth when they applied for a social security number. Perhaps the employer took the social security number application form and they wanted the employer to think that they were younger.

If you did something like that, do not be afraid to tell Social Security. They will not hold it against you. They are only looking to resolve the discrepancies in the evidence.

PROOF OF MARRIAGE RULES

Section 411

To establish your marriage when this is required for entitlement to benefits, Social Security may require your marriage certificate. Of course, marriages are usually recorded and there must be an explanation if you cannot obtain a certificate. You will usually be required to produce a statement from the Bureau of Vital Statistics to the effect that a search was made for your marriage and that no record was found.

If there is no record of your marriage, you may establish using it Secondary Evidence. The oldest and best evidence is recorded for a purpose that would require information about marriage, such as a passport or a child's birth certificate that shows the names of the parents. Statements from your husband's relatives may also be obtained. (See Section 207.5 for a discussion of the marriage requirement.)

SPECIAL PROBLEMS FOR BUSINESS OWNERS

Section 412

If you own your own business, whether you are self-employed or have set it up as a corporation, you encounter special problems when you claim Retirement Benefits from Social Security. Of course, if you are closing up your business altogether, or if you are selling it to a third party who is not a relative, and you will have no further involvement in the business, you should not have a problem.

Social Security almost always requires a face-to-face interview if you own your own business. You cannot usually file a claim over the phone. The reason for this is that Social Security wants to question you in detail about your business and determine how credible you appear. The interviewer will make a written determination about whether he believes you are telling the truth.

If you are not selling your business to a non-relative or are not closing up shop but are claiming Retirement Benefits based on a decrease in earnings, you will have to give a complete and thorough explanation of why your earnings are decreasing. It is not enough to simply cut your salary down on the books. That means absolutely nothing to Social Security.

They will want to know what duties you are performing now that you are claiming partial retirement. They will want to see whether or not the earnings that you report are consistent with the duties that you perform. They will want to know who is performing the other duties now that you are not performing them yourself, and what qualifications they have. It is not enough to say simply, "my wife will run the business," if she has never been involved in the operation of the business.

If you tell Social Security that you will not go to work on certain days, you can be sure that they will send somebody to your place of business on those days to confirm that you are not there. A Social Security representative may pose as a customer.

You will also be asked to give names and addresses of your major customers and suppliers, because Social Security will contact them to verify that you are no longer dealing with them or that your business is off.

Social Security will require your personal tax returns for the last two or three years as well as the business tax returns. They will want to see whether you are taking income from the business and calling it something other than earnings.

For instance, if your business is in the corporate form and your salary is cut, but your dividends from the business increase, they will look to see why that is. You may be disguising salary as dividends.

They will also look at your deductions to see if any of them are being overstated to hide income. When you make your initial application, Social Security will take a very detailed statement from you about the operation and management of your company.

Be prepared when you make your application to give a complete explanation and to thoroughly explain why your earnings will be less than they were before.

Processing Time

Section 413

In general, it takes about two weeks for an application to be processed for payment. At times it can take as little as one week. Unfortunately, in rare cases it can take months and in some cases can take four or five months. Delays can occur if there is a problem with proof of your age or some other requirement, such as marriage.

If your first check does not arrive within three months of the time you give Social Security all the information and documents required, you may have a right to what is called an *expedited payment.* (see Sec. 1013.)

NOTE: *The checks will not be paid until they are due. If you file early, you will not receive your first check until after the month for which the first payment is due.*

As noted in Section 1003, checks are paid in arrears. This means that, for instance, the July check is paid on August 3rd. The check you receive on the third day of the month is payment for the prior month.

If your first month of eligibility is September and you have applied in June, you will not receive your first check until October 3rd. If your first month of eligibility is September and you applied in September, you should expect your first check no later than ninety days after you submitted the last required evidence.

The reason that some cases can be processed for payment within two weeks while others take two or three months is that Social Security has a special computer system that sometimes allows the personnel in the local District Office to make the computer entries to pay the case. Not all cases can fit within this computer system, however, and some cases require approval in a Program Service Center. (see Sec. 102.) This usually adds to the processing time.

WITHDRAWAL OF APPLICATION

Section 414

You can withdraw your filed application at any time before a determination is made on the application. If SSA has already made a determination on the application, it can only be withdrawn if any other person who would lose benefits because of the withdrawal consents to the withdrawal in writing and all benefits that have already been paid on the application are returned to SSA. If SSA approves a request to withdraw an application, it will be treated as though it were never filed.

A request for a withdrawal of an application must be in writing and filed at the Social Security District Office. The usual case in which someone wants to withdraw an application occurs when that someone has applied for reduced Retirement Benefits before sixty-five. He or she later resumes working or earns more than anticipated, so no benefits are payable due to the amount of the annual earnings.

In that case, it would be to his or her advantage to withdraw the application so that the reduction for age would be eliminated in the event that benefits later became payable before sixty-five. Of course, at sixty-five your benefit will be re-figured to exclude the reduction factor for any months for which you did not receive a full monthly benefit. (see Sec. 704.4.)

You may also wish to withdraw an application if you use a "non-service" (see Sec. 804) month in one year, but may be eligible for more non-service months in a later year.(see Sec. 408.)

Eligibility for Medicare coverage is not affected by withdrawal of an application.

DISABILITY BENEFITS: SPECIAL PROVISIONS 5

IN GENERAL

Section 501

There are three different kinds of Social Security benefits that are paid on account of disability. The most common and well known is the Disability Insurance Benefit. (see Sec. 203.) This is the benefit paid to disabled workers. The amount of the benefit is the same as if you were sixty-five.

To be eligible for the Disability Insurance Benefit you must be specially insured. (see Sec. 604.) You must have not only worked long enough under Social Security, but you must have worked in the recent past.

The other Social Security benefits paid on account of disability are Disabled Adult Child Benefits (see Sec. 205.3) and Disabled Widow Benefits. (see Sec. 204.6.) These benefits are paid to children of retired, disabled or deceased workers, and to widows age fifty to fifty-nine. See Chapter 2 for the eligibility requirements.

This chapter will not discuss all the aspects of proving a claim for disability benefits because they are too numerous and complicated. An entire book would be required to cover everything. We will discuss the medical requirement only in general terms. If you should file a claim for disability and be denied, you should hire an attorney to represent you. (see Chapter 13.)

We will discuss in detail those special rules that are unique to disability benefits, other than the medical requirements.

DEFINITION OF DISABILITY

Section 502

As noted in the section above, this book cannot go into a detailed discussion of all the medical requirements for disability benefits. In this section we will discuss the medical requirements only generally.

If you believe that you are disabled, you should file an application for benefits. If you are denied after your first application you should consult an attorney. Many cases that are denied are awarded on appeal. The rules regarding the medical requirements are very complex and you should have a lawyer represent you if you appeal. (see Chapter 13.)

There are three kinds of disability benefits: Disability Insurance Benefits (for disabled workers), Disabled Adult Child benefits (for children of retired, disabled, or deceased workers who become disabled before age twenty-two), and Disabled Widow Benefits (for widows between ages fifty and fifty-nine who are disabled). See Chapter 2 for the exact eligibility requirements for these different kinds of benefits.

For disabled workers and disabled adult children, the law defines disability as the inability to do any kind of substantial gainful activity (see Sec. 504) for a continuous period of at least one year or to result in death. The cause of disability can be either mental or physical, but it must be medically determinable. This means that there must be a medical basis for the condition.

Statutory blindness is also considered a disability. Statutory blindness is defined as central visual acuity of $^{20}/_{200}$ or less in the better eye with the use of glasses, or a limited field of vision in which the widest diameter subtends an angle no greater than twenty degrees. The one year duration requirement also applies to blindness cases.

For disabled widows, the definition of disability is now the same as just stated. Before 1991, the law had a different and stricter requirement. A disabled widow must have been unable to do *any* gainful activity.

NOTE: *For the worker or child the requirement is an inability to do* substantial *gainful activity. As a result of this difference in definition of disability, it was much harder to qualify as a disabled widow. The one year duration requirement (or expected death) also applies in widows' cases.*

The Social Security Administration (SSA) will consider your age, education, and work experience along with your medical condition. This means that even if your medical condition does not prevent all type of work, you may still be eligible if your particular situation, considering age, education, and work background, is such that you cannot be expected to perform the only work you are physically able to do.

The simplest example of this is the laborer in his late fifties who has a back condition that prevents him from performing his regular job. He has done exclusively this type of work. Although he may still have the physical ability to do light work, SSA will consider him disabled because of his age and limited work background.

> ***Warning:*** The rules on proving disability are very complex. If you are unable to do your regular work you should file a disability application. If your claim is denied, consult an attorney and consider an appeal. Many cases that are denied the first time are won on appeal.

THE EARNINGS RECORD "FREEZE"

Section 503

When you are entitled to Disability Insurance Benefits, you are also entitled to what is called a "freeze" because of its effect on your earnings record. The months or years during which you are entitled to a period of disability will not be considered for purposes of calculating benefits.

For instance, if you were disabled for five years during your fifties, when you reach retirement age and apply for Retirement Benefits, the five years of disability will be excluded. This is important because Retirement Benefits are based on your average earnings over many years. If these years of disability were considered, your average earnings would be much lower because you had no earnings during the disability.

Whenever you are eligible for Disability Insurance Benefits, a "freeze" is placed on your earnings record for that period. This happens even if no disability benefits are actually paid, so long as you meet all the requirements. Of course, it is very rare to be eligible without actually being paid.

When we say "eligible" in this section, we mean being officially determined eligible after making an application, as opposed to being potentially eligible. The usual situation in which someone is eligible for a period of disability but receives no benefits is when the disability is based on blindness and the beneficiary is engaging in Substantial Gainful Activity (SGA). See Section 504.1 below for this special case.

The disability freeze applies to the computation of all benefits, not just retirement. It also applies when determining the number of quarters of coverage required. (see Sec. 601.)

SUBSTANTIAL GAINFUL ACTIVITY

Section 504

Regardless of your medical condition, if you have done work during a time you claim disability benefits, you will not be eligible if the work is determined to be Substantial Gainful Activity (SGA), unless you are in a trial work period (see Sec. 509) or it is an unsuccessful work attempt. (see Sec. 506.) If you are an employee, rather than self-employed, the most important factor in determining whether the work is Substantial Gainful Activity is the amount of your earnings.

SSA has established dollar amounts of earnings to use as guidelines. Beginning with January 2001, these monthly amounts are calculated based on the national average wage index.

In 2002, the monthly amount is $780. If the earnings average above this amount per month, the work is considered SGA. If they average below this amount, the work is not considered SGA.

There are different amounts for blind persons. (See Sec. 504.1 in the next section.) The SGA amount will be increased if the wage index rises, but will never be reduced below the prior year's level.

If the earnings show that you are engaging in SGA, you will not be eligible for benefits, no matter what your medical condition may be (See Sec. 509—Trial Work Period and Sec. 506—Unsuccessful Work Attempt.)

Earnings derived from doing volunteer work in programs under the Domestic Volunteer Service Act and the Small Business Act will not be considered when calculating earnings for SGA.

SSA will also disregard any part of your pay that is not based on your actual services.

Example: You may be working for an employer who is subsidizing part of your pay, as in the case of some sheltered workshops. The employer may be paying more than your work performance is worth economically. The amount of any such subsidy will be deducted from your earnings for the purpose of using the earnings guides discussed above.

If the employer does not set a specific amount for such a subsidy, SSA will investigate the circumstances to determine how much of your pay you actually earn and how much represents a subsidy.

Likewise, SSA will deduct from the amount of your earnings any unusual work-related expenses. These expenses, , must be incurred because of your impairment. They only will be deducted if they exceed normal work-related expenses. The expenses will not be deducted if you need them—even if you are not working—such as expenses for medication.

If you are self-employed, SSA will not consider the income you earn as the only test of whether you are engaging in SGA. Your earnings could be affected by any number of factors other than your disability. If your work activity, considering the time devoted to the business, the skills required, duties, responsibilities, efficiency and energy output is comparable to the work activity of non-disabled people in your community, the work will be considered SGA. If not, then SSA will look to the value of your services to the business.

If the value of your services is clearly equal to the monetary guidelines for employees discussed above, the work will be considered SGA. When deciding the value of your services, SSA will look to how much you would have to pay an employee to perform them. If the value of your services is worth less than the monetary guideline for an employee, then SSA will consider the income you get and whether you render significant services to the business.

If you render significant services and the income you derive is equal to or higher than the monetary guideline for an employee discussed above, (even if the value of your services is worth less), the work will be considered SGA. If the income is less than this guideline, but the livelihood you earn is comparable to what you earned before you became disabled, or is comparable to what non-disabled self-employed people in your community derive as a means of livelihood, it will be considered SGA. Your services to the business are considered significant if:

- you are the sole proprietor;

- if you contribute more than half of the management time to the business; or

- if you spend more than 45 hours a month on management time, even if that is less than half of the total management time.

❒ Section 504.1 Substantial Gainful Activity— Special Rules for the Blind

If your disability is based on blindness (see Sec. 502), you will be eligible for monthly benefits even if you are working as long as your monthly earnings do not average more than $1,300 in 2002. This amount will be adjusted in future years based on the national average wage index.

If you have shown an ability to earn amounts equal to the above, your disability benefits will be terminated. However, if you are fifty-five or older your benefits will not be terminated if your present work is not comparable to the work you did before you became blind. If your new work requires skills and abilities less than or different from those that you used before, your benefits will only be suspended for months in which you have earnings over those listed above.

The difference between termination of benefits and suspension is discussed in Chapter 10. If your benefits are only suspended, then you can have them started again without re-applying, and without meeting the one-year duration of disability requirement. (see Sec. 502.)

If you meet the eligibility requirements for disability based on blindness (see Sec. 502), including the work requirement (see Sec. 604), you are eligible for a period of disability, called a *freeze* (see Sec. 503), even if you are performing SGA. Although no monthly benefits are paid while you are working or able to work, you are entitled to the advantage of the earnings record freeze. You must file an application for this and meet all the requirements, as if you were applying for monthly benefits.

THE DATE OF ONSET

Section 505

The date that your disability begins is very important. This date determines how your benefit is computed (see Sec. 702.2), how much work you need, and when. (see Sec. 604.) It determines when the waiting period (see Sec. 507) begins and whether you can receive retroactive benefits. (see Sec. 406.2.)

Your waiting period begins with the first full month of your disability. If you become disabled on the first day of a month, that month will be the first month of the waiting period. If you become disabled on the second or later day of a month, then the next month will be the first month of the waiting period.

For example, if you become disabled on June 10, your waiting period begins with July. If you become disabled on June 1, June is the first month of the waiting period.

The earlier your date of onset, the better it is for you. Your waiting period will end that much sooner so that benefits can start with an earlier month.

If your onset is an earlier year, you may require fewer work credits, or quarters of coverage (see Sec. 604), and your benefit amount will usually be slightly higher. And the further back you can go for retroactive benefits (see Sec. 406.2), the more money can be paid for past due benefits when your claim is awarded.

The date of onset is determined by the date your disability actually began, regardless of whether or not your salary continued.

For example, if you became disabled on June 10, but your salary was paid until December 20, your date of onset is June 10, not December 20, as long as you actually stopped working in June. If your medical condition started before you stopped working, the time you stopped working is used, not when the condition started.

When we say "work" in this section, we mean SGA. (see Sec. 504.) If you are disabled and return to work, but must stop again because of the disability, the date of onset will be the second time you stopped work, unless your return to work can be considered an unsuccessful work attempt. (see Sec. 506.)

For example, you become disabled for the first time in January. You are out of work for the entire month of January, but return to your job on February 15 and work until June 15, when you again stop work, this time for good. Unless the work period from February to June is considered an unsuccessful work attempt (see Sec. 506), your date of onset will be July. If the work period from February to June is determined to be an unsuccessful work attempt, your date of onset is considered to be January.

If you are out of work for an entire year before returning, you may be entitled to a closed period of disability. (see Sec. 508.)

THE "UNSUCCESSFUL WORK ATTEMPT"

Section 506

As noted in Section 504.1 above, the date of onset of your disability is very important. The earlier your onset, the better it is for you. People who have stopped working because of a disability but have then returned to work before stopping work again may be able to use the earlier date as the date of onset.

For example, if you become disabled and do not work at all in the month of January, but then return to work in February and work until April 15, when you finally stop working you may be able to establish January as your date of onset.

A period when you return to work may be considered an unsuccessful work attempt if it lasts less than three months and you are forced to stop work again because of the physical or mental conditions imposed by your disability. You must still meet the medical requirements of disability as of the first time you stopped working. The first period of disability must have lasted a full month or longer, and there can not have been any medical improvement during the time you went back to work.

A period of work can still be considered unsuccessful if it lasts longer than three months as long as all the conditions discussed above are present and, in addition, the work period does not last more than six months ,and there are special considerations given by the employer. The work performance for the six months must be less than is required of non-disabled workers.

You may have more than one unsuccessful work attempt, as long as there is at least one full month of disability between them and there has been no medical improvement.

THE WAITING PERIOD

Section 507

There are no benefits payable to either the disabled worker or any of his dependents for the first five full months of disability. No benefits are payable during the waiting period, nor will benefits be payable later for any months within the waiting period. The waiting period begins with the first full month of disability after the date of onset. (see Sec. 506.)

No waiting period is required if you were previously entitled to disability benefits within the five-year period before your current disability. The waiting period is the first five full months of a period of disability. If you become disabled on the second or later day of the month, that month will not count towards determining your period of disability.

For example, if you become disabled on April 15, the first full month of disability will be May, and the waiting period will start counting with the month of May, so that May, June, July, August, and September will be the months chargeable to the waiting period, and no benefits will be payable for those months. The first month of entitlement to a monthly benefit in that case will be October. The month you become eligible for the payment of the monthly benefits is called your *date of entitlement.*

The waiting period is only used to determine when the monthly benefits should begin. You must still meet the one year duration requirement mentioned in Section 502, unless the disability is expected to result in death.

You do not have to wait until the end of the waiting period before filing an application for disability. You may file for disability benefits at any time after you stop working because of disability. If you file for disability benefits before your waiting period is up, no benefits will be paid until the waiting period has passed.

If it appears from the nature of your disability that it will be permanent or will exceed one year, then it is a good idea to file the application as soon as you stop working, because the application will usually take two to three months to be processed and approved. If the waiting period passes during the time the application is being processed, your benefit checks can begin right away.

Example: You become disabled on April 15, and it appears that your disability will be permanent. The waiting period will be the first five full months of disability, namely May, June, July, August, and September.

If you apply for your disability benefits during your waiting period, let us say in June, and it takes three months (until September) for the application to be approved, you will get your first disability check as soon as it is payable. The month of entitlement will be October and you will receive your check for October on November 3. (Checks are paid in arrears; see Sec. 1003.)

If you wait for the waiting period to pass before making your application, remember that the processing time usually takes up to three months. You will be without benefits during the processing time. Of course, if the claim is approved, the first payment will include any past due benefits payable after the waiting period.

In the example just discussed, if you instead wait to apply until November and it takes three months, until February, for the claim to be approved, you will be without your benefit payments for those months. However, when the first check comes, it will include payment for October, November, December, and January. (see Sec. 1002.)

THE CLOSED PERIOD OF DISABILITY

Section 508

As noted in Section 502, you may be eligible for a disability benefit if your disability lasts for at least one year. An application for disability benefits may be retroactive for up to one year. (see Sec. 406.2.) If you were disabled for at least one year, but since have returned to work, you may be eligible for disability benefits for the period of disability even if you did not file for the benefits at the time. This past period during which you were disabled is referred to as a *closed period* of disability. You will be eligible for the payment of benefits only for months within the twelve-month retroactive life of a disability application. (see Sec. 406.2.)

Example: You become disabled on April 15, 1999, and you recover on June 15, 2000. You return to work at your regular job. You do not file an application for disability benefits until February 2001. The waiting period (see Sec. 507) starts running from the first full month of disability, which is May 1999. It runs from May through September.

Your first possible month of entitlement to a disability benefit is October 1999, and your last month of possible entitlement to a disability benefit is August 2000. (see Sec. 513.) However, because you do not apply until February 2001, your application can be retroactive for only twelve months, which brings it back to February 2000.

Since at the time of application you have recovered from your disability, the period of time that you were disabled is referred to as a closed period of disability. If the claim is approved, you will be paid retroactive benefits for the months of February 2000 through August 2000.

If you had applied for the benefits no later than October 2000, you would have received the benefits for all the months which would be payable, namely from October 1999 (the first month of entitlement) through August 2000.

THE TRIAL WORK PERIOD

Section 509

After you have become entitled to disability benefits you can attempt to work without having your disability benefits immediately terminated if you are still medically disabled. This is referred to as a trial work period. It is different from the unsuccessful work attempt discussed in Section 506. The trial work period only applies after you have become entitled to disability benefits, but the unsuccessful work attempt applies to work periods previous to your application.

The purpose of the trial work period is to allow a disabled beneficiary who is still physically disabled to try to work without penalizing him. Earnings during a trial period have no effect on benefits, even if they exceed the earnings limits that apply to other kinds of benefits. The Work Test (see Sec. 801) does not apply to disability benefits.

You are not eligible for a trial work period if you have made a medical recovery from your disability or if your medical condition has changed to the extent that you are no longer totally disabled, even if you are partially disabled. You must still meet all the medical requirements of total disability to be eligible for a trial work period.

If you are eligible, then your work, even if it is SGA (see Sec. 504 above), will not be considered in determining whether or not your benefits should be cut off. Of course, if the work activity you are performing is not SGA, then your benefits will continue. For 2002, only months for which you have earnings totalling more than $560 will count towards the trial work period. For 2001, the monthly amount was $530.

You are allowed a total of nine months for the work period. After this, your work activity will be evidence that you are no longer disabled.

The nine months of the trial work period do not necessarily have to be consecutive. If you use up two months of the trial work period, stop working altogether for a while, and then work for another two months, you will have used up four months of the trial work period and will have five months remaining.

Example: You become entitled to disability benefits in January 2000. In December 2000, you obtain part time employment and earn $600 per month from December 2000 until March 2001. This work activity is below the earnings guidelines described in Section 504 and, therefore, does not constitute SGA. It has no effect on your disability benefits but it does use up four of your trial work period months because it is over $530 per month.

However, in April 2001 you begin earning $800 per month. This is SGA because it exceeds the earnings guidelines of Section 504. You continue to earn $800 per month from April 2001 through June 2001. You have now used up seven months of your trial work period.

You stop working in June and have no earnings until September 2001, at which time you again begin earning $600 per month, and you continue earning at that rate from then on. Your trial work period months are December 2000 through June 2001 and September and October 2001. That is nine months.

NOTE: *To be eligible for the trial work period, your medical condition must still constitute a total disabil-*

ity. If your medical condition improved, you would not be entitled to the trial work period.

If you continue working and earning above the SGA guidelines (see Sec. 504) after the expiration of your trial work period, then your work activity indicates that you are no longer disabled, regardless of your medical condition. Accordingly, your disability will cease with the first month of SGA (see Sec. 504) after the trial work period expires. You receive an additional two checks after the month that your disability is determined to have ceased. (see Sec. 513.)

THE REENTITLEMENT PERIOD

Section 510

The reentitlement period is an additional thirty-six month period after nine months of trial work during which you may continue to test your ability to work if you continue to have a disabling impairment. You will be paid benefits for months during this period in which you do not perform SGA, but you will not be paid benefits for any month after the first three during which you do perform such work.

If anyone else is receiving monthly benefits based on your earnings record, that individual will not be paid benefits for any month during the reentitlement period for which you cannot be paid benefits. If your benefits are stopped because you perform SGA, they may be started again without a new application and a new determination of disability if you discontinue your SGA during this period.

In determining, for reentitlement benefit purposes, whether you do SGA during a month, SSA considers only your work or earnings for that month; they do not consider the average amount of your work or earnings over a period of months.

THE EFFECT OF WORKERS' COMPENSATION BENEFITS

Section 511

If you receive Social Security disability benefits and also receive Workers' Compensation benefits due to an on-the-job disability, your Social Security benefits may be affected.

If the combination of Social Security benefits (including benefits for your wife and children) plus the amount of the Workers' Compensation benefits you receive per month is greater than eighty percent of your Average Current Earnings, then your Social Security benefits will be reduced so that the total will come down to the 80 percent level. Benefits payable to dependents will be reduced first.

For example let us say that your Social Security disability benefit is $500 and that you have a child under age eighteen who is entitled to $250. You are also eligible for Workers' Compensation benefits in the amount of $450 per month. The total of these benefits is $1,200.

Let us say that your Average Current Earnings before your disability were $1,000 per month. Eighty percent of this is $800 per month.

Because the combination of the Social Security benefits and the Workers' Compensation benefits is $1,200, and 80 percent of the Average Current Earnings is $800, the difference, $400, must be subtracted from your Social Security benefits.

This $400 will be deducted as follows: The dependent's benefit of $250 would be entirely eliminated, and $150 would be taken from your disability benefits.

When determining the Average Current Earnings, Social Security considers the gross amount of your prior earnings, not your net amount after deductions. The Average Current Earnings are calculated in three different ways. Whichever way will give you the highest average is used.

The *first* method of figuring the Average Current Earnings is to take the average monthly earnings during any *one* calendar year within the year of your onset of disability or the five preceding years.

The *second* method of determining the Average Current Earnings is to take the average monthly earnings in any *five* consecutive calendar years after 1950.

NOTE: *The five years must be consecutive. You cannot pick any five after 1950; they must follow one after another.*

The *third* method of determining Average Current Earnings is to take the average monthly earnings of *all* years used in computing the disability benefit. (see Sec. 702.2.)

Whichever of the three methods produces the highest average per month will be used. It is important to note that for purposes of determining Average Current Earnings, your actual earnings are used even if they exceed the amount of earnings subject to FICA tax for that year. Because your earnings record only shows the earnings in a calendar year that are subject to the FICA tax, it is important, if your yearly earnings for a particular year exceeded the FICA maximums, to bring this to the attention of the SSA.

Example: The maximum earnings subject to FICA in 2001 is $80,400. Even if you earn over that amount, usually only the FICA amount will be recorded on your earnings record.

Example: If you earn $100,000 in 2001, for purposes of determining your Average Current Earnings, the $100,000 figure will be used, not the amount shown on your earnings record.

A listing of the FICA maximum for all years is located in Appendix 3.

The Workers' Compensation offset does not apply if the Workers' Compensation Law under which you are receiving Workers' Compensation benefits provides that *compensation* benefits will be reduced by the amount of Social Security benefits you receive.

If the total of the Social Security benefits payable on the individual's earnings record is greater than 80 percent of the Average Current Earnings, then this higher figure is used to figure the offset, instead of the 80 percent figure.

For example, if the Average Current Earnings are $1,000 per month, 80 percent is $800. If the total amount of benefits payable on the account, including the dependents, is $900 per month, then the Social Security benefits will be reduced so that the combination of Workers' Compensation and Social Security benefits do not exceed $900.

It is rare, however, that the total Social Security benefits exceed 80 percent of Average Current Earnings.

THE EFFECT OF OTHER KINDS OF BENEFITS OR PAYMENTS

Section 512

Benefits paid under private disability insurance policies have no effect on Social Security disability benefits. Employee salary continuation will not have any effect, nor will any back pay, retroactive increases past due, commissions or any other such payments from an employer. Besides Workers' Compensation, discussed in Section 511, the only type of disability benefits that affect your Social Security disability are those that are required by any federal, state, or local law.

For example, some states have laws that require employers to pay disability benefits to disabled employees. Such benefits offset Social Security disability benefits in the same way as Workers' Compensation. These benefits are added to the amount of Workers' Compensation and the computation of the offset is then the same. You should note, however, that if the statute requiring the special disability benefit provides for an offset for Social Security benefits, then this offset provision does not apply.

WHEN THE DISABILITY BENEFITS END

Section 513

There is a difference between *cessation* of disability and *termination* of disability benefits. Cessation of disability occurs when

Social Security determines that you are no longer totally disabled within their definition of disability. (see Sec. 502.) Termination of benefits occurs two months after cessation of disability.

For example, if Social Security determines that your disability ceased in June, your disability will terminate as of August. You will receive the benefits for June, July, and August, but not thereafter.

Cessation of disability occurs when your medical condition is no longer considered to be totally disabling or when you begin performing SGA. (see Sec. 504.)

Social Security conducts periodic reviews of many Social Security disability cases in order to reconsider the medical condition of the beneficiary. If, after such a medical review, Social Security determines that your condition is no longer totally disabling, your disability is considered to have ceased. It is the policy of the SSA to send you a notice of this determination, and if they fail to do so, your disability will not be considered to have ceased until as you receive the notice.

Example: Say that SSA conducts a medical review of your case and determines that, based on your medical records, your disability has ceased as of June 19, 2001. However, due to office problems, they do not mail the notice to you until August 2001. It is SSA's policy to make your official cessation of disability in August, the month you receive the notice, rather than June, the month that they determine that your medical evidence no longer is considered totally disabling.

Even if your medical condition remains the same or worsens, if you are performing SGA (see Sec. 504), your disability will be considered to have ceased.

NOTE: *If you are entitled to a trial work period (see Sec. 509), your work activity will not be considered SGA until nine months of the trial work period have passed. You may then be entitled to further benefits for non-work months. (see Sec. 510.)*

NOTE: *Not all work activity is considered SGA. (see Sec. 504.)*

THE CONTINUING DISABILITY REVIEW

Section 514

SSA conducts periodic reviews of disability cases to determine whether you are working and whether your medical condition has changed. Some cases are reviewed more frequently than others, and some cases are not reviewed at all. It depends on the nature of your disability. When your claim is first awarded, a date is usually set at that time for a future review.

You will be notified when your case is being called for review, and generally you will be called to the District Office to give current information about any work activity you may be doing, to obtain the names of your current doctors and any recent periods of hospitalization. SSA may have you examined by one of their consultant physicians, at their expense.

If you do not cooperate with this continuing disability review, Social Security has the authority to stop your disability benefits because of your failure to cooperate.

INSURED STATUS: 6
THE WORK
REQUIREMENT

THE WORK REQUIREMENT IN GENERAL

Section 601

To qualify for a Social Security benefit, either you or the person on whose earnings record you claim benefits must have worked a certain amount of time in employment covered by Social Security. Almost all employment in the U.S. is now covered. The work requirement is called *insured status*.

There are different kinds of insured status, depending on the type of benefits being claimed. *Fully insured* status (see Sec. 602) is required for most benefits. *Currently insured* status (see Sec. 603) is required for Young Widows (see Sec. 204.5) and surviving children. (see Secs. 205.1-205.4.) A special *disability insured* status (see Sec. 604) is required for Disability Insurance Benefits. (see Sec. 203.)

Dependents and survivors are eligible based on relationship to an insured worker. There is no work requirement for them. The person on whose account benefits are claimed must meet the applicable insured status requirement.

The eligibility requirements for the different kinds of benefits are listed in Secs. 202-207.2. Each listing states the insured status requirement for the particular benefit.

The insured status requirement does not affect the amount of the benefit. It sets a minimum work requirement which must be met before any benefit is payable. Once this minimum is met, a benefit amount is computed based on average earnings. (see Chapter 7.)

If you have insured status on your own and also qualify as a dependent or a survivor, you may be entitled on both accounts. (see Chapter 3.)

Insured status is gained by earning Quarters of Coverage. (see Sec. 605.1.) These are calendar quarters for which credit now is given based on certain minimum earnings during the year.

FULLY INSURED STATUS

Section 602

Fully insured status is required for most benefits. To be fully insured, you must earn one Quarter of Coverage (see Sec. 605.1) for every year after 1951 up to and including the year you turn sixty-two (for Retirement Benefits), become disabled (for Disability Insurance Benefits) or die (for Survivor Benefits).

NOTE: *There is an additional requirement for Disability Insurance Benefits (see Sec. 604), and that certain Survivor Benefits do not require fully insured status. (see Sec. 603.) For Survivor and Disability Benefits, the rule is different if the worker was born after January 1, 1930. Instead of 1951, use the year of attainment of age twenty-two.*

Social Security considers you to have attained your age on the day before your birthday. For example, if your birthday is

January 1, 2001, you become sixty-two on December 31, 2000. Therefore, if your birthday is January 1, you attain age twenty-two or sixty-two in the year before that birthday for purposes of figuring the insured status requirement.

To collect wife's, widow's, or child's benefits you do not have to meet the work requirement yourself. Instead, you must be the wife, widow, or child of a worker who meets the requirement.

The minimum number of Quarters of Coverage required in any case is six. The maximum is forty.

To compute the quarters required for Retirement Benefits, subtract 1951 from the year you become sixty-two. For Survivor or Disability benefits, use the year of death or onset of disability (see Sec. 506) instead of the year you turn sixty-two, if this is earlier, and the year of attainment of age twenty-two instead of 1951 if this is later.

A chart that lists the quarters required for fully insured status depending on year of attainment of age sixty-two, disability, or death is located in Appendix 2. It applies to those born on or before January 1, 1930.

Example: John was born on August 11, 1950. He became disabled on June 5, 1994. We add twenty-two to the year of birth (22+1950=1972). John attained age twenty-two in 1972. We subtract 1972 from the year of onset of disability (1994-1972=22). John needs twenty-two Quarters of Coverage (see Sec. 605.1) to meet the fully insured part of "disability insured" status. (see Sec. 604.)

CURRENTLY INSURED STATUS

Section 603

This type of insured status requires fewer Quarters of Coverage (see Sec. 605.1) than fully insured status. (see Sec. 602.) However, only some kinds of benefits can be based on currently insured status. These are:

- Surviving Child's Benefits (see Secs. 205.1-205.4);

- Mother's Benefits (see Sec. 208, also called *Young Widow's Benefits*);

- the Lump Sum Death Benefit (see Sec. 207.2); and

- Medicare for kidney failure cases (see Sec. 207.3).

A worker must earn at least six Quarters of Coverage (see Sec. 605.1) within the thirteen calendar quarter period ending with the calendar quarter of death. The calendar quarters are as follows: first quarter—January, February, March; second quarter—April, May, June; third quarter—July, August, September; fourth quarter—October, November, December.

To determine this period, take the quarter and year of death and subtract three from the year; the period begins with the quarter of the resulting year which corresponds to the quarter of death.

Example: Jim died on May 15, 2001. This is in the second quarter of 2001. We subtract three from 2001 to get 1998. The thirteen quarter period begins with the second quarter of 1998 and ends with the second quarter of 2001. If Jim earned six Quarters of Coverage (see Sec.

605.1) during that period, including the beginning and ending quarters, he is currently insured.

DISABILITY INSURED STATUS

Section 604

Eligibility for Disability Insurance Benefits (see Sec. 203) requires a special "disability insured" status. You must be fully insured (see Sec. 602) and meet a second requirement of recent Quarters of Coverage. (see Sec. 605.1.) This second requirement is different depending on when you become disabled.

If you become disabled in or after the calendar quarter during which you turn age thirty-one, you must have at least twenty Quarters of Coverage (see Sec. 605) during the forty calendar quarter period ending with the quarter your disability begins. (see Sec. 505.) To determine this period, subtract ten from the year the disability begins and begin with the first quarter after the quarter in the resulting year that corresponds to the quarter of onset of disability. (The calendar quarters are on page ___ under "Section 603.")

Example: John becomes disabled on September 5, 2001. This is the third quarter of 2001. Subtracting ten from the year bring us to 1991. The corresponding quarter of that year is the third quarter. The forty-quarter period begins with the first quarter following the corresponding quarter. Therefore, the period begins with the fourth quarter of 1991 and ends with the third quarter of 2001. If John has twenty Quarters of Coverage within this period, including the beginning and ending quarters, he will meet the second part of the "disability insured" status requirement.

Sometimes the requirement is referred to as the "five year" rule or the "five year out of ten year" rule. This is somewhat misleading. Although twenty quarters is five years and forty quarters is ten years, the legal requirement is based on quarters, not years. The twenty quarters required do not have to be consecutive, they can be spread out. The forty-quarter period does not always correspond to the beginning and ending of calendar years. This rule is more accurately called the $^{20}/_{40}$ rule, i.e. twenty quarters required in the forty-quarter period.

If you become disabled before the calendar quarter of your thirty-first birthday, there is an alternative to the $^{20}/_{40}$ rule. Instead, you must have one Quarter of Coverage (see Sec. 605.1) for every two calendar quarters in the period beginning with the calendar quarter after the quarter of your twenty-first birthday and ending with the quarter of onset of disability. (see Sec. 505.)

If the number of quarters in this period is an odd number, use the next lower even number. A minimum of six quarters of coverage is always required. Quarters of Coverage earned before age twenty-one may be used if this is necessary to meet the requirement.

If you were disabled before age thirty-one and received benefits based on the alternative to the $^{20}/_{40}$ rule just discussed, but then your disability ceased, and you become disabled again after age thirty-one, you will meet the disability insured status requirement. You will do so even if you cannot satisfy the $^{20}/_{40}$ rule as long as you have at least one Quarter of Coverage for every two calendar quarters beginning with the quarter after attainment of age twenty-one and ending with the quarter of the new onset date. You exclude any quarter wholly or partially within the prior period of disability, except for the beginning or ending quarters if they are Quarters of Coverage.

In all cases, you must be fully insured. (see Sec. 602.)

QUARTERS OF COVERAGE

Section 605

❏ Section 605.1 Quarters of Coverage in General

A Quarter of Coverage is a calendar quarter for which credit is given by Social Security for purposes of deciding if a person has worked long enough to qualify for benefits. (see Sec. 601.) A minimum amount of wages from covered employment or self-employment income must be earned to get credit. Almost all employment and self-employment is now covered by Social Security. The amount of earnings required to get credit has changed. The rules are discussed in the following sections of this chapter.

❏ Section 605.2 Quarters of Coverage—Pre 1978 for Employees

In years before 1978, you receive a Quarter of Coverage for each calendar quarter during which you were paid $50 or more. It does not matter when the wages were earned. The Quarter of Coverage is assigned to the quarter in which the wages were paid to you. However, if you were paid maximum yearly earnings subject to Social Security, (the FICA maximum), you are given credit for the four quarters of that year, even if the earnings were paid in less than four quarters. The yearly FICA maximums are listed in Appendix 3.

There is a special rule that applies to farm workers for years before 1978. Instead of the $50 per quarter rule, a farm worker received one Quarter of Coverage for each $100 in cash wages paid during a year, without regard to the quarter in which the wages were paid. Quarters of Coverage were assigned beginning with the last calendar quarter and then counting backward.

Beginning with 1978, the rules for all employees have been changed. (see Sec. 605.3.) The rules have always been different for the self-employed. (see Sec. 605.4.)

❏ **Section 605.3 Quarters of Coverage—Post 1977 for Employees**
Beginning with 1978, Quarters of Coverage are assigned based on total yearly earnings instead of earnings paid within a calendar quarter. A certain amount has been designated for each year, and one Quarter of Coverage is credited for each multiple of that amount which is paid within the year. These amounts are listed in Appendix 2, Chart 1.

Example: John was paid $800 in 1984, when the required multiple was $390. He is credited with two Quarters of Coverage because his earnings were at least two multiples of $390, but less than three multiples. Jim was paid $1,600 in 1984. He receives four Quarters of Coverage because his earnings are at least four multiples of $390.

No more than four Quarters of Coverage are given for one calendar year. A Quarter of Coverage cannot be assigned for any quarter that has not yet started, nor for any quarter that begins after the worker's death.

❑ Section 605.4 Quarters of Coverage for the Self-Employed

The method of determining Quarters of Coverage for self-employed individuals is different than it is for employees. Before 1978, the self-employed person received four Quarters of Coverage for a year if the net earnings from self-employment were $400 or more. If the net earnings from self-employment were less, the self-employed did not receive any Quarters of Coverage. It was all or nothing.

Beginning in 1978, the rules changed. For 1978 and all later years, a self-employed person receives Quarters of Coverage based on the amount of total yearly earnings in the same way as an employee. (see Sec. 605.3.)

However, the self-employed individual must still meet a minimum of $400 in net earnings from self-employment to receive any Quarters of Coverage.

Example: John works as a plumber for the Smith Plumbing Company. He earned $350 in wages in 1978 . He receives one Quarter of Coverage, because this is more than the minimum required earnings for one Quarter of Coverage as discussed in Section 605.3.

Joe, however, is a self-employed plumber. His net earnings from self-employment in 1978 were $375. He receives no Quarters of Coverage even though his net earnings from self-employment are greater than the minimum earnings required for an employee.

If he had earned $400 in self-employment income in 1978, he would have received one Quarter of Coverage. If he had earned $400 in net earnings from self-employment in 1977, he would have received four Quarters of Coverage.

If you are both self-employed and an employee, add your total earnings as an employee and your net earnings from self-employment to determine how many Quarters of Coverage you will receive using the rule described in Section 605.3. However, to include any net earnings from self-employment into the yearly total they must total at least $400. If the net earnings are less, they are not added in at all.

Example: Joe is both self-employed as a plumber and works as an occasional employee of Smith Plumbing Company. In 1978 he had $400 in net earnings from self-employment and $350 in wages. Combining the two sums equals $750. Using the rule described in Section 605.3, he earns three Quarters of Coverage. If the earnings and self-employment income were reversed, the outcome would be different.

If he had $400 in wages but only $350 in net earnings from self-employment, he would receive only one Quarter of Coverage. The net earnings from self-employment are less than $400 and do not get added in at all; only his wages count. Because his wages are only one multiple of the minimum required for 1978 ($250) he receives only one Quarter of Coverage.

BENEFIT AMOUNTS 7

In General

Section 701

For obvious reasons, the way that the Social Security Administration (SSA) computes the amount of benefits payable is very important to everyone. In this chapter we will discuss the rules that are used to figure benefits. We will discuss the basic computation, recomputation due to earnings after you first become entitled to benefits, reductions for age and for entitlement to other benefits, and the credits given for delayed retirement.

Deductions because of earnings are discussed in detail in Chapter 8. The method and the timing of payments are discussed in Chapter 10.

COMPUTATIONS

Section 702

❏ Section 702.1 The Primary Insurance Amount

The first step in figuring benefits is to determine the primary insurance amount (PIA). All benefits are based on it. The benefit amounts for a retired worker at age sixty-five and for a disabled worker are equal to the PIA. It is reduced for retirement benefits before sixty-five and increased for delayed retirement.

Benefits for spouses, children, and survivors are figured as a percentage of the PIA. The PIA is the single most important concept for computing benefit amounts.

❏ Section 702.2 The Basic Computation Formula

The PIA is based on the earnings of the worker on whose account the benefits are claimed. PIAs for workers with maximum, high, average, and low lifetime earnings are listed in Appendix 4.

There is one basic formula used to compute almost all PIAs. Some special formulas, used rarely, are discussed in Section 702.3. The basic formula is described in this section, but is extremely complicated and is almost always done by SSA's computers, rather than manually.

The 1978 amendments to the Social Security Act mandated "indexing" of earnings to adjust earnings of earlier years for inflation occurring now. The first step of the basic computation formula is to index the worker's annual earnings for past years. Each year's earnings are separately indexed.

To do this, SSA first determines the *indexing year*. For retirement cases, this is the second year before the year the worker becomes age sixty-two (not necessarily the year of retirement). For disability cases it is the second year before the onset of disability, and for survivor cases it is two years before the year of death. For example, for a worker who becomes age sixty-two, disabled, or dies in 2001, the indexing year is 1999.

SSA then determines the *average annual earnings* of all workers for the indexing year and for each past year after 1950. They divide the average earnings of all workers for the indexing year by the average earnings of all workers for each prior year. They multiply the answer for each year by the amount of the worker's earnings for that prior year (but not more than the FICA maximum for that year). The result is the indexed earnings for each prior year. This process is for all years after 1950 up to, but not including, the indexing year. SSA uses actual earnings, not indexed earnings, for the indexing year and later years.

After the earnings for all years have been indexed (except for the indexing and later years), SSA then determines how many years to use for the computation.

For people born before 1930, subtract 1951 from the year of attainment of age sixty-two, onset of disability, or death—whichever is earliest. (People who become disabled at age sixty-four should still subtract 1951 from age sixty-two because that is earlier than the onset of disability.)

For people born in 1930 or later, add twenty-two to the year of birth. Subtract that figure from the year of attainment of age sixty-two, onset of disability, or death. For retirement and survivor benefits, subtract five. The result is the number of years used, called *computation years*.

For disability benefits:

- if the onset of disability is age twenty-six or younger, do not subtract anything additional;

- ages twenty-seven through thirty-one, subtract one;

- ages thirty-two through thirty-six, subtract two;

- ages thirty-seven through forty-one, subtract three;

- ages forty-two through forty-six, subtract four;

- age forty-seven or older, subtract five.

The minimum number of computation years used is two. The maximum number of computation years is thirty-five.

Example: John becomes sixty-five in 1997. This means that he turned sixty-two in 1994. Subtract 1954 from 1994. The answer is forty. You then deduct five. The result is thirty-five. Use thirty-five computation years to figure John's PIA.

Example: Bill was born in 1947 and died in 1993. Add 22 to 1947. The result is 1969. Subtract 1969 from

1993. The answer is 24. Deduct 5. Use 19 computation years.

Example: Joe was born in 1951 and became disabled in 1994 at age forty-three. He turned twenty-two in 1973. Subtract 1973 from 1994. The answer is twenty-one. Deduct four. Use seventeen computation years.

After determining the number of computation years, SSA looks at the annual indexed earnings calculated as described above, from 1951 through the year before the year for which the benefit is calculated. You may include the year of death in survivor cases. Take the computation years with the highest indexed earnings, and add up the total indexed earnings for those computation years.

When recomputing a retirement benefit to include earnings after entitlement, the number of computation years is the same. If the earnings for the new year are higher than the indexed earnings of the lowest year used in the first computation, substitute the new year's earnings. When you add the new year's earnings to the total, you must subtract the lowest year's indexed earnings.

Once SSA has determined the total indexed earnings for the computation years, they divide by the number of months in the computation years. These are called *Divisor months*. The number of computation years times twelve equals the divisor months used.

The total of the indexed earnings for the computation years used, divided by the divisor months, rounded to the next lower dollar, yields the *average indexed monthly earnings*.

The PIA is a certain percentage of the average indexed monthly earnings. This varies depending on the average indexed monthly earnings and on the year for which the computation is being done. For example, for 1992, the percentages are as follows: 90 percent of the first $387, plus 32 percent of the excess more than $387 up to $2,333 of the average indexed monthly earnings, plus 15 percent of the average index monthly earnings more than $2,333.

The dollar amounts at which the percentages change are called *bend points*. The percentages (90 percent, 32 percent, 15 percent) stay the same for each year, but the bend points change annually. They are determined by dividing the indexing year's average total wages of all workers by the average total for 1977 ($9,779.44), and multiplying the result by $180.00 and $1,085.00 to give you the two bend points.

The bend points used depend on the first year of eligibility (i.e. the year the worker becomes sixty-two, disabled, or dead), and remain applicable for later recomputations, even though the recomputation is done in a later year.

Cost-of-Living Adjustments (see Sec. 704.2) are added to the PIA beginning with the year of eligibility, effective with the month of increase.

Once the primary insurance amount is calculated, the benefit amount payable is determined according to the rules in this chapter, and by referring to the benefit amounts listed for each type of benefit in Chapter 2.

❐ Section 702.3 Other Computation Formulas

The basic computation formula discussed in the preceding section applies to almost all beneficiaries. Other computations are used in a very small number of cases, which we will discuss briefly.

The 1977 amendments to the Social Security Act changed the basic computation formula to the average *indexed monthly earnings* method discussed in Section 702.2. The general effect of this change was to take inflation into account, but also to reduce the amount of benefits.

For workers who turned sixty-two before 1984, Social Security may use a different formula. This other formula is called the *new-start transitional guarantee*. When using this formula, however, Social Security does not add in earnings from the year you attained age sixty-two or later. This formula does not use indexed earnings; instead, it uses the actual earnings. The transitional guarantee formula may result in a higher PIA in some cases in which the last year's earnings were in 1980 or 1981.

If you had been entitled to Disability Insurance Benefits more than a year before your entitlement to Retirement Benefits, the year of your death in survivor cases, or a second period of disability, you will receive the higher of a PIA figured under the basic computation formula or the PIA upon which your disability benefit was based. In other words, you will not have a lower PIA than you had while you were disabled.

SSA also uses other formulas when there are little or no earnings after 1951. We will not discuss the details of these other formulas, but you should be aware that they may be used. As noted above, only a very small number of people will have a higher benefit under these other computation formulas. Social Security will automatically consider all computation formulas and give you the highest one.

❐ Section 702.4 The Effect of Having Years With No Earnings

As noted in Section 702.2 above, the years used in figuring the PIA are the years from 1951 or the year that you turn twenty-two, if later, through the year before the year that you turn age sixty-two. The lowest five years are dropped from that base period.

If you have five or less years with no earnings shown on your earnings record, it will have no effect on your computation. However, if you have more than five years with no earnings, then it will, because the overall average monthly earnings during the computation will be less.

Generally, if the year with no earnings is a later year, it will have more of an effect than an earlier year. This is because the amount of earnings covered by Social Security have increased over the years, so that recent years' earnings subject to FICA (see Appendix 3) are very high, although "indexing" (see Sec. 702.1) has somewhat reduced the disparities.

❐ Section 702.5 How to Double-Check Your Benefit Amount

In the vast majority of cases, Social Security correctly computes your benefit amount, but sometimes mistakes occur.

The most common mistake is the failure to include earnings for a given year. If earnings are not shown on your earnings record, it may affect the amount of your average monthly earnings and, therefore, the amount of your benefit.

If you doubt the accuracy of your benefit amount, the first thing to do is to go to your Social Security office and ask them to obtain a copy of your earnings record used in the computation of the benefit. It may take them several weeks or a month to do so.

You should check to make sure that the correct earnings are posted for each year. If there is a year that does not have earnings shown, determine if it makes a difference in the computation of your benefit. If it is one of the five lowest years in the computation period as discussed in Section 702.1 above, then it does not matter.

The general rule is that you can correct your earnings record only for the past three years. However, there are exceptions to this rule. (see Sec. 1405.) If you have a year with no earnings shown that is more than three years in the past, you can ask Social Security to re-check their records in Baltimore. This is called a *scout*.

If earnings turn up on the *scout*, your benefit will be re-adjusted. If they do not turn up, Social Security may still allow you to correct your earnings record if you have evidence of the earnings, such as W-2 form, pay stubs, or a tax return.

If all of your earnings are shown on your earnings record and you still doubt the accuracy of the benefit, you should ask a

Claims Representative (see Sec. 105) to show you, step by step, how your benefit was computed.

If you are not satisfied, you have the right to request a reconsideration. This is part of the administration appeals process. (see Chapter 13.)

REDUCTIONS

Section 703

❒ Section 703.1 Reductions for Age—Benefits Before Age Sixty-Five

In General

In the case of retirement, aged wife's, aged widow's and disabled widow's benefits, your benefit amount will be reduced if you take the benefit before Full Retirement Age, which is age 65 for those born before 1938. (1940 for widows.) The reduction is figured on a monthly basis, not yearly.

Beginning in 2003 (but affecting those turning 62 in 2000), Full Retirement Age will gradually increase, in two-month increments per year, to age 66 by 2009. There will then be an eleven-year pause. The increases will then resume, going to age 67 by 2027.

This change affects those persons turning age 62 beginning in 2000. The effect of the change is that the benefit at age 62 is reduced more than previously (by 5/12 of 1 percent for each extra month).

The following chart contains the full retirement age for workers and spouses born after 1937 (for widow's see section on page 166):

If the birth date is...	Then full retirement age is...
1/2/38-1/1/39	65 years and 2 months
1/2/39-1/1/40	65 years and 4 months
1/2/40-1/1/41	65 years and 6 months
1/2/41-1/1/42	65 years and 8 months
1/2/42-1/1/43	65 years and 10 months
1/2/43-1/1/55	66 years
1/2/55-1/1/56	66 years and 2 months
1/2/56-1/1/57	66 years and 4 months
1/2/57-1/1/58	66 years and 6 months
1/2/58-1/1/59	66 years and 8 months
1/2/59-1/1/60	66 years and 10 months
1/2/60 and later	67 years

There are different reduction formulas for retirement, wife's, and widow's benefits. These are discussed in detail in the following sections.

Reduction for Age—Retirement Benefits

If you are entitled to a retirement benefit before the month you reach Full Retirement Age, the benefit must be reduced. The reduction factor goes by months, not by years, so that if your first month of entitlement is the month before Full Retirement Age, the benefit is reduced by 1 month. If the first month of entitlement is 6 months before Full Retirement Age it will be reduced 6 months and so forth all the way back to age 62 (but see Section 207.4 dealing with the "throughout the month" rule).

The legal reduction factor is 5/9 of one percent of the PIA for each month of the first 36 months you are entitled to a benefit before the month you reach Full Retirement Age. The factor for each month of reduction in excess of 36 months is 5/12 of 1 percent. This applies to individuals whose full retirement age is after age 65. A 36-month reduction comes out to 20 percent but remember that the reduction factor goes by month, not by year.

Example: If you were born in September 1934, you turned 65 in September 1999. If your entitlement to benefits started in January 1998 your PIA is reduced by 20 reduction months because that is the number of months before the month you turn 65. If your PIA is $500.00, 1 percent of it is $5.00. 5/9 of 1 percent is $2.77. Multiply this amount by the number of reduction months. 20 times $2.77 is $55.40. The monthly benefit amount is $500.00 minus $55.40, which is $444.60.

Please note that if your Full Retirement Age is over 65 (see previous chart above), extra reductions are applied for each month in excess of 36. The actual amount payable to you is rounded down to the nearest dollar ($444.00). (see Sec. 705.7.)

A third method of figuring the reduced benefit is to use the reduction factor listed in the chart in Appendix 5. The factor for twenty reduction months is .888. Using the above example, multiply .888 by 500 (the PIA) to arrive at a monthly benefit amount of $444.

You may note that there are some minor discrepancies in the results obtained by using the above formulas. The first formula is from the Social Security Act, the second is the one Social Security uses, and the third is the one published in Social Security pamphlets.

Please note that any reduction for age stays in effect until you turn sixty-five. At that time, the reduction factor is readjusted to exclude any reduction for months before sixty-five for which you do not receive a full monthly benefit. (see Sec. 704.4.) If you receive all monthly benefits, the reduction stays in effect for life.

Reduction for Age—Spouse's Benefits

Benefits payable to a spouse of a retired or disabled worker are reduced if entitlement to the spouse's benefit begins before the month the spouse reaches Full Retirement Age. See the preceding subsection on retirement benefits for the new rules for those turning sixty-two in 2000.

Extra reduction months are applied for months in excess of thirty-six. The reduction factor for these excess months for spouse's benefits is the same as for retirement benefits, i.e. $^5/_{12}$ of one percent.

NOTE: *If the wife is entitled because she has a child in her care (see Sec. 207.8), there is no reduction for age.*

The spouse's benefit is reduced only for the spouse who is entitled because of her age. If the spouse has worked under Social Security and is entitled to a retirement benefit on her own account, see Section 302.

The reduction formula applicable to spouse's benefits is $^{25}/_{36}$ of one percent of one-half of the worker's PIA for each of the first thirty-six months of entitlement to the spouse's benefit before Full Retirement Age, and $^5/_{12}$ of one percent for months in excess of thirty-six.

The reduction factor goes by months, not by years, so that the difference between taking a reduced benefit when you are sixty-two and eleven months and taking it when you are exactly sixty-three is one additional month of the reduction factor.

Example: Wanda is sixty-three. She never worked under Social Security. Her husband is entitled to a benefit with a PIA of $600.00. Wanda becomes entitled to spouse's benefits when she is fifteen months under age sixty-five.

To figure her benefit amount we take one-half of her husband's PIA ($600.00 divided by two equals $300.00); one percent of $300.00 is $3.00; and $^{25}/_{36}$ of $3.00 is $2.08. Multiply this amount times fifteen reduction months for a figure of $31.20. This is subtracted from $300.00 to result in a monthly benefit amount of $268.80, rounded down to the nearest dollar of $268.00. (see Sec. 705.7.)

Example: Now let us assume that Wanda worked under Social Security and has a PIA of $200.00. Her benefit would be figured as follows.

First we take her own PIA and reduce it by fifteen reduction months using the formula described in Section 708 above. The $200.00 is reduced because of her age to $183.30, rounded down to $183.00.

We then determine her spouse's benefit and reduce it. The spouse's benefit is $100.00 (the difference between one-half of her husband's PIA and her own PIA). It is reduced fifteen months using the formula described in this section. The $100.00 is reduced to $89.50, rounded down to $89.00.

Her monthly benefit amount is composed of her own reduced benefit in the amount of $183.00, plus the reduced spouse's benefit in the amount of $89.00, for a total benefit payable of $272.00.

Instead of using the formula described above, another formula is used by Social Security. The formula is 144 minus the number of reduction months, times one-half of the worker's PIA, divided by 144, rounded down to the nearest dollar, or $[(144\text{-}RM)\times 1/2\ PIA]/144$. Use the difference between one-half

of the spouse's PIA and your own PIA if you are eligible on
your own account.

Another method of figuring the spouse's benefit is to use a
reduction factor from the chart in Appendix 8. Multiply
one-half of the worker's PIA times the reduction factor corresponding to the number of reduction months.

For example, the factor for fifteen reduction months is .895.
To figure Wanda's spouse's benefit from the above example
(assuming she was not entitled to a benefit on her own
account) take 300 (one-half of her husband's primary insurance amount) times .895 to arrive at the reduced wife's
benefit amount of $268.50, rounded down to $268.00.

Please note that the reduction stays in effect for all months
before age sixty-five, but then is readjusted to exclude a
reduction for any month before age sixty-five for which no
full monthly benefit is paid. (see Sec. 704.4.) If all benefits
before sixty-five are paid, the reduction stays in effect for life.

The maximum amount of the reduction for age based on
thirty-six reduction months is twenty-five percent.

Reduction for Age—Widow's Benefits

Widows who are entitled to benefits because of age will
have their benefit amounts reduced for any month before
Full Retirement Age for which they are entitled to a benefit. A disabled widow under sixty receives the same benefit
amount as a widow at age sixty. For benefits payable before
January, 1984, widows who were entitled to disabled
widow's benefits before age sixty have an additional reduc-

tion of $^{43}/_{240}$ of one percent for each month of entitlement before age sixty.

Beginning with those born in 1940 and later, additional reduction months are applied because the Full Retirement Age has been increased above age sixty-five. See the discussion of this at the beginning of this Section. The applicable Full Retirement Age for widows depends on the year of birth according to the following chart:

If the birth date is...	Then full retirement age is...
1/2/40-1/1/41	65 years and 2 months
1/2/41-1/1/42	65 years and 4 months
1/2/42-1/1/43	65 years and 6 months
1/2/43-1/1/44	65 years and 8 months
1/2/44-1/1/45	65 years and 10 months
1/2/45-1/1/57	66 years
1/2/57-1/1/58	66 years and 2 months
1/2/58-1/1/59	66 years and 4 months
1/2/59-1/1/60	66 years and 6 months
1/2/60-1/1/61	66 years and 8 months
1/2/61-1/1/62	66 years and 10 months
1/2/62 and later	67 years

The formula specified in the Social Security Act for widow's benefits is a reduction of 19/40 of 1 percent of the PIA for each month before age Full Retirement Age at the time entitlement begins. This works out to a 28 1/2 percent reduction at age 60 for those born before 1940. This will increase at 0.95 percent for every two months of additional reduction months applied to those born in 1940 and later, according to the chart.

The reduction factor is based on the number of months before age Full Retirement Age, not the number of years. For instance, if you take a reduced widows benefit at age 62 1/2, the benefit will be reduced by 30 reduction months.

The formula used by Social Security to compute the widow's benefit amount is as follows: 4,000 minus (number of reduction months times 19), times the PIA, divided by 4,000, or [4,000-(19xRM)xPIA]/4000.

Regardless of the amount arrived at by using a reduction formula, the widow's benefit can never be greater than the amount of the monthly benefit that the husband received during his lifetime if he was entitled.

Example: If the husband took a fully reduced benefit at exactly age sixty-two, his PIA was reduced. The widow cannot receive more than he received even if she first becomes entitled when she is at Full Retirement Age.

Likewise, any additional credit for delayed retirement (see Sec. 704.6) is added to the benefit of the widow.

Example: If the husband had a primary insurance amount of $500.00 which was increased by 3 percent due to delayed retirement, the widow's benefit would be figured using $515.00, the increased amount. At Full Retirement Age the reduction factor is readjusted to exclude any reduction for a month before Full Retirement Age for which no full monthly benefit was actually paid. (see Sec. 704.4.)

NOTE: *A widow also receives a readjustment of the reduction factor at age sixty-two. (see Sec. 704.5.)*

If a widow is entitled to a benefit based on her own account at age sixty-two, she has an option to take either the reduced widow's benefit or the reduced retirement benefit on her own account and then switch over to the other benefit unreduced at Full Retirement Age or earlier. (see Sec. 303.)

How Taking Reduced Retirement Benefit Will Affect Other Benefits

If you take a retirement benefit before age sixty-five and it is therefore reduced for age, it may have an effect on other benefits payable to you or to others. The most common example of this is the case of widow's benefits. If you take your own reduced retirement benefit and then die, the amount your widow may receive cannot exceed the amount you were receiving in your lifetime, although she is older than age sixty-five at the time she first becomes entitled. She will, however, receive any cost of living adjustments that may occur after your death.

If, at the time you apply for reduced retirement benefits, you are also potentially eligible for spouse's benefits on a husband's or wife's account, you must apply for the reduced spouse's benefit as well, even if, there are no benefits actually payable because of the husband's or wife's earnings.

This provision only applies if, at the time you make your application for reduced retirement benefits, your spouse is entitled to retirement or disability benefits.

Example: Your spouse turned sixty-five last year and is entitled to retirement benefits and Medicare. However, due to his earnings, no benefits are payable.

You are sixty-two years old now and you apply for your own reduced retirement benefit. Social Security will require you to file an application for the reduced spouse's benefit if one half of the spouse's PIA is greater than your own PIA, regardless of whether cash benefits are payable to you as a spouse (your spouse's earnings will have no effect on the payment of your own benefits).

If your spouse retires in two years, the additional spouse's benefit will be paid at the reduction rate in effect at the time you first applied for your own retirement benefits, and not based on your age at the time the benefits are first payable, until you become sixty-five when the reduction will be adjusted. (see Secs. 414 and 704.4.)

If you are potentially eligible for widow's benefits at the time you file for reduced retirement benefits, you do not necessarily have to apply for them. You have the option of taking one or the other benefit reduced and then switching over to the other one unreduced at age sixty-five. (see Sec. 303.)

If you apply for reduced retirement benefits and you have a spouse who may be entitled on your account, the fact that your benefit is reduced for age has no bearing on determining the amount of the spouse's benefit. The spouse's benefit will be reduced according to his or her age at the time of the first entitlement. Your PIA will be reduced for the number of months you are under sixty-five at the time of first entitlement; for the spouse, one half of your PIA will be reduced by the number of months he or she is under sixty-five at the time he or she becomes entitled. (see Sec. 703.1.)

If you become entitled to disability insurance benefits, the amount of your disability benefit will be reduced by the number of months you receive a retirement benefit before receiving a disability benefit.

For example, let us say that you become disabled at age sixty-three. No benefits are payable for the first five full months of the waiting period of your disability. (see Sec. 507.) Because you are more than sixty-two, you may receive reduced retirement benefits during the waiting period. The amount of that benefit is reduced for your age at the time you first become eligible for the retirement benefit. If you are exactly age sixty-three at that time, the PIA is reduced by twenty-four months using the reduction formula described in Section 703.1 above.

When you become entitled to the disability benefit after your waiting period, the benefit amount will be readjusted to exclude reduction for any months for which you have not received a retirement benefit. Your disability benefit is reduced, but only by the number of retirement benefits you received before becoming eligible for disability benefits.

Other benefits payable to dependents on your account will not be affected by the fact that you take reduced retirement benefits.

How Taking Reduced Widows Benefits Will Affect Your Own Benefit

If you take a widow's benefit before age sixty-five it will not affect benefits on your own account if you were born after 1928. You may switch over at age sixty-five to your own unreduced benefit, if that will yield a higher amount. This is discussed in full in Section 303.

However, if you were not born after 1928 and take a reduced widow's benefit before age sixty-two, it may have a permanent effect on your own retirement benefits. The dollar amount of that reduction will be deducted from your own PIA at age sixty-five.

If you take your own benefit before sixty-five, only one reduction will be imposed, either the regular retirement reduction (see Sec. 703.1), or the dollar amount of the widow's reduction caused by receipt of widow's benefits for any month before age sixty-two, whichever is higher. (see also Sec. 704.5.)

❒ Section 703.2 The Family Maximum

If there are dependents entitled to benefits on your account, there is a maximum amount payable to your family unit, regardless of what the full payment amounts to the dependents would be individually. This is referred to as the *family maximum*.

For example, in the case of a retired worker who has three children under eighteen entitled on his account, each child's benefit without taking the family maximum into account would be fifty percent of his PIA. However, depending on the size of his PIA, there is a maximum that can be paid to the family, regardless of the number of beneficiaries.

Once this maximum is reached, it does not matter how many additional dependents are entitled on the account, because the total amount payable on the earnings record cannot exceed the family maximum. Each dependent's benefit is reduced proportionately so that the total for everyone does not exceed the family maximum. The worker's own benefit is never adjusted for this purpose.

The amount of the family maximum depends on the type of benefit you receive and the year in which you become sixty-two, become disabled, or die, i.e., the *year of eligibility.* The family maximums are the same for retirement cases and for survivor cases. There is a different family maximum for - disability cases.

In the case of retirement and survivor accounts, the family maximum goes on a sliding scale. The scale varies depending on the year of eligibility. *Bend points* are used in the same way that a PIA is derived from average indexed monthly earnings. (see Sec. 702.2.)

The family maximum is 150 percent of the PIA up to the first bend point, plus 272 percent of the excess of the PIA over the first bend point up to the second bend point, plus 134 percent of the excess of the PIA over the second point up to the third bend point, plus 175 percent of the PIA in excess of the third bend point.

The percentages (150 percent, 272 percent, 134 percent, 175 percent) remain the same from year to year, but the bend points will change in the same way as the bend points used to compute the PIA. (see Sec. 702.2.)

In disability cases, the family maximum is 85 percent of the average indexed monthly earnings (see Sec. 702.2), but not more than 150 percent of the PIA, nor less than 100 percent of the PIA.

Once the amount of the family maximum is determined, the dependent's benefits are reduced proportionately so that the total family benefits do not exceed the maximum. In the case of retirement and disability benefits, the worker's PIA (not the benefit amount after age reduction) is deducted from the family maximum, and the balance is divided among the dependents, in a proportion according to their original benefit amounts before any age reduction, as is the case with survivor benefits.

The adjustment for the family maximum is made after any deductions. (See Sec. 705 of this chapter.) If a dependent is not receiving benefits because of work deductions, the adjustment is made as if that dependent is not entitled on the account.

When a person is entitled as a child on more than one account, the family maximums of both accounts are combined.

A divorced spouse's or a divorced widow's benefit is not reduced for the family maximum. Other dependent's benefits on the account are not reduced due to a divorced spouse's or widow's entitlement on that account.

RECOMPUTATIONS

Section 704

❐ Section 704.1 Recomputations in General

At the time you first apply for Social Security benefits, a PIA is computed (see Sec. 702.2) and a benefit amount determined.

This may be adjusted later under certain circumstances. Adjustments to the PIA or monthly benefit will affect benefits payable beginning with the effective date of the adjustment.

There are four basic types of recomputations: cost of living increases, adjustments to include earnings after you first become entitled to a benefit, reduction factor adjustment at sixty-two and sixty-five, and the delayed retirement credit that increases your benefit if you do not receive monthly benefits after age sixty-five. These are discussed in detail in the following sections.

❐ Section 704.2 Cost of Living Increase

Each year all Social Security benefits are increased according to the cost of living increase that occurred in the preceding year. This is based on inflation as reflected in the

Consumer Price Index. The cost of living increase is effective beginning with the month of December.

NOTE: *Monthly benefits are paid in arrears (see Sec. 1003) so that the benefit increase effective with December is reflected in the monthly benefit check received in January of the following year.*

The cost of living increases are shown in Appendix 5. The increase is computed as a percentage of the monthly benefit amount, not the PIA.

❑ Sec. 704.3 Adjustment for Earnings After Entitlement

As noted in Section 702.2, the PIA is based on your earnings ending with the year before the year you first become eligible (survivor cases include the year of death).

For example, if you apply for benefits in 1999, your earnings through 1998 will be included in the computation. However if you work in the year you first become entitled to benefits or later and the earnings in the later, year are greater than the lowest year's earnings in the computation of your benefit, then your PIA will be increased. If the amount of your earnings in the later year is less than the lowest year's earnings, there will be no increase in your benefit. (see Sec. 702.2.)

The increase is effective with January of the year after the year of the additional earnings. If you continue working, and your annual earnings are greater than the lowest year used in the computation of your benefit, the increased benefit amount will be payable beginning with January of the following year.

This adjustment increases your PIA and accordingly will increase the benefit for anyone who is receiving benefits on your account.

Social Security will automatically readjust your benefit amount to include additional earnings if it yields a higher benefit. However, they are very backlogged in doing this. In fact, they run years behind. You may request an earlier readjustment.

☐ Section 704.4 Refiguring the Age Reduction at Full Retirement Age

If you received a benefit reduced for age (see Sec. 703.1), the reduction factor will be adjusted effective with the month you reach Full Retirement Age. This adjustment will eliminate the reduction for any month before Full Retirement Age for which you did not receive a full monthly benefit. If you received all benefits, there will be no adjustment. If you received a partial benefit for a month, the reduction attributable to that month's entitlement will be eliminated because you did not receive a *full* monthly benefit.

This reduction factor adjustment applies to all benefits that were reduced for age and is effective beginning with the month you reach Full Retirement Age. It cannot be figured until after the year of Full Retirement Age because the amount of your earnings may affect whether or not any benefits will be withheld for that year.

Example: John filed for reduced retirement benefits to be effective fifteen months before Full Retirement

Age. Accordingly, his PIA was reduced by fifteen months. After he became entitled to reduced retirement benefits, he had earnings that prevented the payment of benefits for six full months and for part of a seventh month.

When he reaches Full Retirement Age, the PIA will be reduced permanently by only eight months. The month he received partial payment is also eliminated. His benefit amount will increase accordingly. No adjustment will be made until after he files an annual report (see Sec. 902.3) for the year he reaches Full Retirement Age.

When the recalculation is done, it will be retroactive to the month he reaches Full Retirement Age.

❑ Section 704.5 Refiguring Age Reduction for Widows at Age Sixty-Two

In addition to the reduction factor adjustment at sixty-five as described in Section 704.4, widows who received reduced widow's benefits before sixty-two are entitled to a readjustment of their benefit amount at sixty-two.

This readjustment is to eliminate a reduction factor for any month before sixty-two for which they did not receive a full monthly benefit. The increased monthly benefit will be payable beginning with the month they turn sixty-two.

Example: Sally applies for widow's benefits at exactly age sixty, and the widow's benefit is therefore reduced by sixty reduction months. She returns to work and has earnings that require five monthly benefits to be withheld and part of a sixth month before sixty-two. The reduction factor based on sixty reduction months will be used to figure benefits payable up through the month before she becomes sixty-two.

However, beginning with the month she turns sixty-two, the reduction factor will be adjusted to eliminate the six months for which she did not receive a full monthly benefit before sixty-two. If she works again between sixty-two and sixty-five, the benefit amount will be adjusted again at sixty-five, as described in Section 704.4.

❏ Section 704.6 Delayed Retirement Credits

If you continue to work after Full Retirement Age and your monthly benefits are withheld because of your earnings, you will receive a credit for each month (beginning with the month you reach Full Retirement Age) for which you did not receive any monthly benefit. The credit varies, depending on your year of birth, from $1/4$ of one percent to $2/3$ of one percent for each month beginning with the month of attainment of Full Retirement Age for which you did not receive any monthly benefit. This comes out to between three percent and eight percent per year.

The chart in Appendix 12 lists the percentages according to year of birth. The credit is payable beginning with January of the year following the year in which you did not receive the benefits. In addition to the delayed retirement credit, you may also be eligible for an adjustment because of your earnings after your first year of entitlement. (see Sec. 704.3.)

The delayed retirement credit will not affect the benefits of any dependents on your account, but if you die and leave a widow, the widow will be entitled to the delayed retirement credit.

You are eligible for the credit whether or not you file at sixty-five. It will be computed when you start to receive benefits. No credit is granted for any period during which you are not fully insured. (see Sec. 602.)

❐ Section 704.7 How to Expedite Adjustments for Earnings after Entitlement

As discussed in Section 704.3, the amount of your benefit may be increased if you have earnings after the first year you become eligible for benefits, provided that those earnings are higher than the lowest year of earnings used in the computation of your benefit amount.

The increase due to earnings is payable beginning with January of the year following the year of the earnings.

Social Security will recompute this adjustment automatically. However, it will take them many months and probably years to do it. This is because there is a lag from the time you earn the wages until the time Social Security receives the report of your earnings and then acts on it to increase your benefit.

You can expedite this process by making a special request. To do this, you will need your W-2 form (or tax return for the year if you were self-employed). You must go or write to your local District Office and show them your tax return or W-2. Ask that the earnings be refigured immediately instead of waiting for the automatic readjustment. Social Security will act upon your request and refigure your benefits, although it may take several months.

Whether you ask Social Security to do it immediately or wait until they do it automatically, the adjustment will be retroactive to the first month after the year for which you had the earnings.

DEDUCTIONS

Section 705

❒ Section 705.1 Deductions in General

After your monthly benefit amount is calculated using the rules discussed in this chapter, Social Security may, under certain circumstances, withhold part or all of the monthly benefit. The major reasons for these deductions are discussed in the following sections.

NOTE: *The family maximum discussed in Section 703.2, may also cause a reduction of the amount of the benefit payable to a dependent or a survivor.*

The deductions we discuss here apply to the actual benefit amount figured after taking into account any reductions for age or adding any credits for later earnings or delayed retirement. Additionally, you may elect to have income tax deductions made from your benefits. (see Sec. 1409.)

❏ Section 705.2 Deductions Because of Earnings

If your earnings in a year during which you are entitled to monthly benefits are over the limits applicable to that year, then some or all monthly benefits must be withheld. The retirement test, or the work test, as it is sometimes called, is discussed in full in Chapter 8. Once the amount of benefits to be withheld is determined by using the annual earnings test, full monthly benefits for that year will be withheld beginning with the first month during which you are entitled, unless you request prorating. (see Sec. 803.)

For example, if, based on your annual earnings and application of the work test, it is determined that $5,000 of monthly benefits must be withheld and your monthly benefit amount is $600, then your monthly benefit will be withheld until the $5,000 is reached. If you are eligible beginning with January to a monthly benefit of $600, then benefits for the months of January through September will be withheld in full. This would be $4,500 worth of benefits. An additional $500 must be withheld to satisfy the $5,000, therefore the benefit for the month of October will have the $500 deducted and only $100 will be payable to you.

If you first became entitled to benefits beginning with the month of June instead of the month of January, no monthly benefits would be payable to you at all for the year because 7 x $600 is only $4,200, which is less than the amount that must be withheld based on your annual earnings.

If you have dependents entitled on your account, the dependents' benefits will also be withheld if your earnings require.

(see Sec. 803.) However, the earnings of a dependent will affect only that dependent's benefits and will not affect the benefits of anyone else who receives payments on the account.

☐ Section 705.3 Deductions from Disability Benefits for Worker's Compensation or Disability Payments

If you are entitled to a disability benefit and are also entitled to Worker's Compensation or certain other types of disability payments (see Secs. 511-512), the combination of the Social Security benefit and Worker's Compensation benefit (or other disability payment that is subject to the offset provision) cannot exceed eighty percent of your average earnings. The way average earnings are figured for these purposes is discussed in Section 511.

The offset will also apply to any dependents who receive benefits on your account, offsetting their benefits before yours.

For example, your average earnings were $1,000 per month; you are entitled to a $500 Social Security disability benefit; and you have a child who is entitled to $250 on your account. You are also eligible for $350 per month in Worker's Compensation benefits. Eighty percent of your average earnings is $800, but the total of the Social Security benefits and the Worker's Compensation benefits is $1,100.

Therefore, the $300 difference must be withheld. First, the child's benefit will be withheld, then $50 of your own benefit, so that the total of the Social Security benefits and Worker's Compensation benefits does not exceed eighty percent of the average earnings.

❑ Section 705.4 Deductions from Spouse's and Widow's Benefits Due to a Government Pension

If you receive Social Security benefits as a wife or a widow, the amount of your benefit is reduced if you receive a government pension based on your own earnings, if the public employment in which you worked was not covered by Social Security.

This government pension offset does not apply if you were potentially eligible for entitlement to a Social Security benefit as a wife or as a widow as of January 1977, and you first became eligible to a government pension from December 1977 through November 1982 (whether or not you received it).

If you were not potentially eligible for the Social Security benefit in January 1977, or if you became eligible for your government pension in December of 1982 or later, one hundred percent of your government pension is deducted from your wife's or widow's benefit.

Due to a change in the law in 1983, if you became eligible for your government pension in July 1983 or later (whether or not you actually receive it) the offset is only $^2/_3$ of the government pension.

These offsets apply only to spouse's or widow's benefits and do not apply to benefits on your own earnings record. The government pension offset applies only if your public employment was not covered by Social Security.

❏ Section 705.5 Deductions to Recover an Overpayment

Overpayments are discussed in detail in Chapter 11. If it is determined that you have been overpaid, you may have to pay the overpayment back. (See Chapter 11 for exceptions.) If you are receiving Social Security benefits, benefits will be withheld to recover the overpayment.

This is discussed in Section 1114. In the first instance, Social Security will advise you that they will withhold your full monthly benefit until the entire amount of the overpayment has been recovered. However, you may request that less than the full monthly benefit be withheld. Generally, this request will be granted if the overpayment can be recovered within three years.

For instance, you were overpaid $1,000 and are entitled to a monthly benefit in the amount of $500. Social Security will seek to recover the overpayment by withholding two months' benefits.

However, you may request that only part of your monthly benefit be withheld to recover the overpayment, and Social Security generally will allow you thirty-six months.

Instead of having the $1,000 deducted from two full months' benefits, the sum of approximately $30 per month may be deducted from your monthly benefits to recover the $1,000 Social Security does not charge any interest on this installment method of paying back the overpayment. (For a more complete discussion of overpayments, see Chapter 11.)

❏ Section 705.6 Deductions for Medicare Premiums

The medical insurance part of Medicare (Part B) requires the payment of a monthly premium. This premium may be higher if you did not apply for Medicare coverage in a timely fashion. (see Sec. 1203.)

If you are covered by medical insurance under Medicare the premium will be deducted from your monthly benefits, if you are receiving them. Otherwise, you will be billed on a quarterly basis. When your benefits begin, the premium will be deducted from the monthly benefit. If you have already paid a quarterly bill, you will receive a refund at a later date.

❏ Section 705.7 Rounding Down

After Social Security computes your benefit (and makes any required deduction), the resulting monthly benefit amount will be reduced to the lowest multiple of $1. Rounding down is done after all the other factors used in computing benefits have been applied, including the Medicare deduction.

The only time that rounding down is not the last step is in the case of combined benefits. (see Sec. 1004.) In that case, each benefit amount is figured separately and rounded down separately. The rounded down amounts are then combined.

EARNINGS LIMITATIONS 8

THE EARNINGS TEST IN GENERAL

Section 801

All beneficiaries, except those whose benefits are based on disability or have attained Full Retirement Age (currently age 65—see Sec. 703.1), are subject to a loss of benefits if their earnings exceed certain limits. The way your earnings affect benefits is called the Work Test, the Retirement Test, or the Earnings Test. They are all the same. Although disabled workers are not affected by the work test, their spouses and children who receive benefits on their account are subject to the test. The effect of a disabled beneficiary's earnings are discussed in Section 504.

If your yearly earnings are below certain annual limits, there is no effect on benefits. If they are over the annual limit, you lose one dollar in benefits for every two dollars over the limit if you are under sixty-five throughout the year, or one dollar for every three dollars over the limit if you are sixty-five or over during the year. The limits are different depending on your age (see Secs. 802.1-802.2), and the year being examined. There is also a monthly limit that usually applies for only one year. (see Sec. 804.) The earnings limits for different years are listed in Appendix 7.

The earnings of a retired worker affect all dependents receiving benefits on his or her account. However, a dependent's earnings will not affect the worker or any other dependent on the same account. Likewise, the earnings of a person receiving survivor benefits will not affect anyone else on that account.

Only earned income is considered for these purposes. (see Sec. 805.) Income such as dividends and interest are not included. (see Sec. 806.) All earnings for the year are counted, even your earnings before you become eligible for benefits or after your entitlement ends. See Section 807 and Section 808 for special rules.

If you have a short taxable year, such as occurs when you switch from a calendar to a fiscal year, the annual earnings limit is prorated in the same way as the year of death. (see Sec. 810.)

EARNINGS LIMITS

Section 802

❏ Section 802.1 Earnings Limit—Under Full Retirement Age

If you will not reach full retirement age during the year, you will lose one dollar of benefits of every two dollars over the annual limit for that year. (see Appendix 6.) All earnings for the year are included, even those earned before your eligibility for benefits. Earnings limits are listed in Appendix 6.

NOTE: *You may receive benefits for any month that your earnings are less than the monthly limit (see Sec. 804), usually for only one year.*

To determine the amount of benefits that must be withheld, subtract the yearly limit from your annual earnings and divide the remainder by two.

❐ Section 802.2 Earnings Limit—Full Retirement Age

Beginning the month you attain Full Retirement Age (FRA), you can earn as much as you like and still collect all your Social Security benefits. For the year you reach Full Retirement Age, if you are an employee, only the amount of money you earn through the month before the month of attainment of FRA will count.

For example, if you reach FRA in July, only your earnings from January 1st through June 30th are included for the work test. You should not report your earnings from July 1 on.

If you are self-employed, divide your annual earnings by 12 and then multiply the answer by the number of months before the month you reached FRA.

Example: Paul attained FRA on August 5, 2000; he was self-employed all year and had net earnings from self-employment of $36,000. Divide the $36,000 by twelve to arrive at the amount of $3,000. Multiply the $3,000 by seven (the number of months in the year before he reached FRA). He should report $21,000 in self-employment earnings, because only this amount will affect benefits.

You lose one dollar in benefits for every three dollars over the annual limit. (see Appendix 6.) To determine the amount of benefits which must be withheld, subtract the yearly limit from your annual earnings, and divide the remainder by three

How Earnings Are Charged Against Monthly Benefits

Section 803

Whenever you earn over the yearly exempt amount, Social Security will withhold the required amount (see Sec. 801) of Social Security benefits beginning with the earliest month of entitlement. Social Security will withhold full monthly benefits until the entire amount that has to be withheld for the year is withheld. (See Sec. 806 for exceptions.)

They do not prorate the withholding over the course of the year (unless you request this—see below), they withhold all benefits beginning with the first month of eligibility, until the full required amount has been withheld.

Example: Harold is sixty-four, and is entitled to $500 a month from Social Security. He expects to have excess earnings requiring $1,200 to be withheld from his Social Security benefits. Social Security will withhold his entire checks for January and February. They will withhold $200 for March, and pay him

$300 for that month. He will receive his full $500 benefit for the months of April through December. All the withholding is done before any benefits are paid to him.

If one or more dependents receives benefits on your account, any partial payment is allocated to each beneficiary proportionate to his share of the total family benefits.

Using the above example, assume Harold had a wife Beatrice, who is older than sixty-five, not working and entitled to $250 a month on Harold's account. The $1,200 to be withheld would be withheld as follows: January—Harold, $500; Beatrice $250; February—Beatrice, $150; Harold, $300. Harold would receive a check for $200 for February and Beatrice would receive a check for $100. Both would receive full checks for March through December.

If Beatrice had excess earnings instead of Harold, only her benefits would be withheld. A dependent's earnings will never require withholding of the worker's or another dependent's benefits. Likewise, the excess earnings of a survivor will not affect another survivor's benefits.

Excess earnings are not carried over to another year. Only the benefits payable in the year of the earnings are subject to withholding. See Section 806 regarding the monthly earnings test.

❏ Section 803.1 Pro-Rating

Although Social Security procedures usually require full withholding of benefits until all required benefits are withheld, you may request that the withholding of benefits be prorated over the course of the year. Instead of receiving no benefits for the normal withholding period, and then the full benefits, you may choose to receive partial benefits.

In the example above, the $1,200 to be withheld could be spread over twelve months at $100 per month deducted from each month's benefits, instead of waiting until March to receive any benefits.

If the period for prorating does not extend into the following year, your written request for prorating will be granted, but not for any period earlier than the month you request it. The amount to be withheld must be at least $25, before the Medicare Part B deduction, if any. Prorating of work suspensions will not be granted if you have an existing overpayment. (see Sec. 1101.)

Prorating may be extended up to June of the following year, but only if you claim that loss of benefits will cause a financial hardship, or require you to significantly revise your retirement plans. Social Security will ask you to explain this in writing. Additionally, there must be no expectation that you will have earnings over the limit in the following year.

In limited situations, you may request that current year work suspensions be deferred completely to the next year.

This request will be granted only if you claim extreme financial hardship unless you receive full payments for a limited time until your financial situation improves. The recovery of the deferred deductions must be accomplished by June of the following year. This request will not be granted if you have an existing overpayment, or if you expect to earn over the limit in the following year.

THE MONTHLY EARNINGS TEST

Section 804

If your earnings for a year are over the applicable earnings limits (see Appendix 6), Social Security will determine the amount of benefits that must be withheld. No benefits will be withheld from a non-service month, no matter how high the annual earnings may be. The way non-service months are determined is called the Monthly Earnings Test.

Under this rule, you have a non-service month for any month after entitlement in which you earn under a certain amount, if you are an employee. If you are self-employed, the test is whether you render substantial services to your business. The monthly limits for employees vary depending on your age and the year involved. Amounts are listed in Appendix 6.

If you are self-employed, the dollar limits do not apply. Instead, the *substantial services* rule is used. Generally, if you spend more than forty-five hours per month at your business, your services are considered substantial. If you work less hours per month, the services are not substantial and you may have a non-service month. If your business is highly remunerative, such as a lawyer, doctor, consultant, etc., more than fifteen hours per month is considered substantial.

You may be eligible for more than one non-service month in a year, but you are not eligible for non-service months in more than one year (with some exceptions to be discussed). The year in which you are eligible for non-service months is called a *grace year*. It is the first year in which you have a non-service month. This is not necessarily the first year you are entitled to benefits.

Example: John turns sixty-five in 1999 and applies for benefits. Although he continues working and earns over the monthly amount in every month of 1999, some benefits are payable, because the amount to be withheld based on his yearly earnings is less than the total of his benefits for the year. (See Section 408 for a discussion of how this works.) Because he has zero non-service months in 1999, this is not a grace year. He has even higher earnings in 2000, enough to require withholding of all benefits. However, he earns under the monthly limit during the months of August and September. Because these are non-service months, he is paid his benefits for those months despite his annual earnings. 2000 is his grace year. He works in 2001, and again his earnings require withholding of all benefits. He has no earnings in July, August, or September, but these benefits are withheld based on his annual earnings because he has already used his grace year.

There are two situations in which certain beneficiaries are entitled to a second grace year. The first case applies to a child, a Young Wife (see Sec. 204.2), or a Young Widow. (see Sec. 204.7.) These beneficiaries receive a second grace year for the year in which their entitlement terminates, unless the termination is due to death or change to another type of benefit with no break in entitlement.

The second case applies to any beneficiary who receives one type of benefit that terminates, but then becomes entitled to another type of benefit with at least a one-month break entitlement. The first year with a non-service month during which the beneficiary is entitled to the second benefit is a grace year.

INCOME THAT COUNTS

Section 805

Under the annual earnings test, your earnings are the sum of gross wages plus net earnings from self-employment, minus any net loss from self-employment.

Wages are counted even if they are not covered by Social Security tax (FICA). Bonuses and awards are counted if they were actually earned during the year. Advances against future commissions are counted if you are an employee.

Dividends and interest received by a dealer in stocks and securities are counted if produced by his inventory for resale. Profit-sharing payments from a plan that is not tax-exempt are included. Real estate dealers who hold property for resale must include rental income from such property.

Royalties received from a copyright or patent obtained in or after the year you turn sixty-five are counted for deduction purposes. However, royalties received from such property obtained before the year you turn sixty-five are not counted, beginning with the year you turn sixty-five.

Sick pay received during the first six months after you stop work is included, as well as temporary disability insurance, unless you paid the premiums for it.

Travel and business expenses paid to an employee are counted, unless they are specifically identified as such at the time the payment is made. Vacation pay is counted, but if it is paid at the time of or after the termination of employment and is attributable to a prior year, it may not be counted for the current year's earnings.

Before 1984, payments of idle-time, standby, "subject to call," and other such payments for a non-work period after age sixty-two were not counted for the work test. Since January 1, 1984, these types of payments have been included as earnings.

INCOME THAT DOES NOT COUNT

Section 806

Payments which do not represent wages or self-employment income are not included for purposes of the retirement test. You do not count such items as interest, dividends, capital gains, legal damages (unless they result from a legal action for wages), wages that are used to hire a substitute employee, rental income, income from a hobby, prizes and awards, royalties from a personally-created work on which you obtained a patent or copyright before the year you turned sixty-five if the royalties are received during or after the year you turned sixty-five, sick pay received more than six months from the last month you worked, unemployment benefits, and worker's compensation benefits.

Certain self-employment income may be excluded. (see Sec. 808.)

Although a particular payment may be considered wages for deduction purposes, if it is attributable to a time before your entitlement it may not affect your benefits. See the next section.

WHEN EARNINGS ARE COUNTED

Section 807

Wages are counted as earnings for the year in which they were earned. It is presumed that wages paid in a particular year were earned in that year, unless you demonstrate otherwise. Self-employment income is earned when received (or accrued, for those on the accrual method), regardless of when the services were rendered.

Sometimes special payments are made at or near retirement, such as advances, back pay, bonuses, severance pay, accrued vacation pay, holiday pay, and so forth. If these payments were earned in an earlier year, they are not included in the earnings test for the year of retirement. Likewise, the month in which such a payment is earned may be important for determining non-service months. (see Sec. 804.)

If your employment has not ended, payments for sick pay, holiday pay, and vacation pay are earned at the time of your absence. Advances against commissions, payment in lieu of vacation, and occasional bonuses are considered earned in the month of payment. If you can establish that they should be attributed to a different period, Social Security will do so. Back pay, regular bonuses and school teachers summer pay are considered earned in the month for which payment is made.

If the payment is made at the time of or after your employment terminates, the wages are considered earned as of the last month worked. However, if it is clear from a written plan that the payment relates to an earlier period, it will not be counted as earnings for the current period.

For example, if you have accrued a month's vacation that you could have taken in an earlier year, you do not include that as earnings for the retirement test when you are paid for that vacation time upon your retirement.

See the next section for a discussion of the self-employment income exclusion.

SELF-EMPLOYMENT INCOME AND LOSSES
Section 808

Net losses from self-employment may be deducted from gross wages and other self-employment income for the year.

Example: Jim is a plumber. He earns $10,000 in wages. He also is self-employed in a plumbing business. He has $7,000 in net losses in his business. Only $3,000 is counted as earnings for the retirement test.

For purposes of the retirement test, you may exclude all self-employment income attributable to services rendered before your first month of entitlement, but received (or accrued, for those who use that method) in a year after the first year of entitlement. For example, if your first month of entitlement is

December, you may exclude from the next year's earnings (for the retirement test only) that income attributable to services performed before December of the year of entitlement.

SPECIAL PROBLEMS FOR BUSINESS OWNERS

Section 809

As a business owner, it is easy for you to reduce your salary when you reach retirement age to qualify for benefits, even if you do not actually retire. Social Security has special procedures for retirement claims from people who own businesses. They will not simply accept your word that your earnings are below the earnings limit.

Social Security will assume that your earnings are over the limit unless you can prove to their satisfaction that your actual services have been reduced.

If you have sold your business, they will want to see the contract and other documents to make sure it is a bona fide transaction and not merely a sham solely designed to make you eligible for benefits.

If you will continue in the business, they will want an explanation of why your income is reduced. Any reduction in income must correspond to a reduction in your services. Stopping or cutting your salary, without a reduction in your duties, is not sufficient. They will want to know who will assume your former duties, and what qualifications that person to do so.

Social Security will require you to give a signed statement detailing the nature of your business, your pre-retirement and post-retirement duties, the names and addresses of your major customers and suppliers, how many hours you will spend at the business and on what days, what kinds of payments you receive from the business, and how much.

They will require you to submit your personal and business tax returns for the last two or three years, and any other records that they deem important, depending on your type of business.

They will check up on the statements you give. They will call your suppliers and customers to see if you are still personally dealing with them. A Field Representative (see Sec. 105) may call at your place of business, posing as a customer, to see if you are there and if you are working. They will scrutinize your tax returns to see if you are overstating deductions or taking money out of the business in a disguised form.

Social Security does all this to prevent payment of retirement benefits to someone who has not really retired. If they decide that your retirement is questionable, they will not pay you.

Before you file for benefits, if you are not selling or closing your business, you must be prepared to explain, in full detail, why your earnings will be less, and who is taking over your duties. Expect them to confirm everything you tell them. Even if they start your checks, they may reevaluate your case in three months, six months, or a year. If they do and then decide that you were never really retired, they may claim that they overpaid you and require a refund.

A consultation with a lawyer with Social Security experience would be wise. You should do this before you go to the Social Security office. You are within your rights to intentionally restrict your earnings to qualify for benefits if you wish, but your earnings must be fairly related to your actual services.

SPECIAL RULE FOR THE YEAR OF DEATH

Section 810

When a beneficiary dies, the annual earnings limit for the year is prorated according to the number of months during which the beneficiary was alive. If the beneficiary dies in the year of his sixty-fifth birthday before the month of that birthday, the under sixty-five annual limit (see Sec. 802.1) is prorated. If he dies in the month of the sixty-fifth birthday (whether before or after the birthday) or later, the over sixty-five limit is used. (see Sec. 802.3.)

Example: William's sixty-fifth birthday is September 27. He dies September 5. His annual earnings limit is $9/12$ of the applicable yearly limit. (see Appendix 6.)

WORK OUTSIDE THE U.S.

Section 811

If you work in a foreign country for seven or more days in any one month, your benefit will be suspended for that month, unless the work is covered by U.S. social security tax. It does not matter how much your earnings are, even if the totals for the year or month are under the regular limits. (see Secs. 801-802.3.) Benefits for any dependent on your account are also suspended.

REPORTING REQUIREMENTS 9

REPORTING REQUIREMENTS IN GENERAL

Section 901

After you have become entitled to Social Security benefits, you must report to the Social Security Administration (SSA) any change that may affect your continued eligibility to receive benefits. For all types of beneficiaries, earnings must be reported if they go over the earnings limits for the year, except in the case of those who receive benefits on account of disability. (See Chapter 8 for a full discussion of the annual earnings limitations.)

In addition to earnings, anything else that affects benefits must be reported, including marriage, remarriage, or divorce, not having a young child in your care for a month, stopping school attendance, or in some cases residing in certain foreign countries. Most common times will be discussed in the following sections.

REPORTING EARNINGS

Section 902

❐ Section 902.1 Reporting Earnings in General

Chapter 8 has a full discussion of the annual earnings limitations. The amount of money you are allowed to earn without any effect on your benefits depends on how old you are and on which year is involved. There are special reporting requirements for disability cases. This is discussed in Section 908 below.

If you receive benefits for another, for example, if a mother receives benefits for a child, it is your responsibility to report the earnings for that person.

Earnings can be reported to the SSA by a telephone call to the local district office, or by a letter. If you have earned over the allowed amount for a year during which you have received benefits, you will be required to file an annual report of earnings. (see Sec. 902.3.)

❐ Section 902.2 When to Report Earnings

When you file a claim for Social Security benefits, you will be asked how much you expect to earn during that year. Additionally, if you file in the last three months of a year, you will be asked to estimate how much you expect to earn in the following year. The benefits paid to you will be based upon your estimates.

Likewise, when you file an annual report of earnings (see Sec. 902.3), you will be asked how much you expect to earn in the coming year, and your benefits will be based on that. If you estimate that you will earn under the exempt amount for a year, you will be paid all benefits due. If you say that you will earn over the exempt amount, Social Security will deduct the required amount from your monthly payments. (see Sec. 803.)

If you later expect that your earnings will be different than what you reported to Social Security, you should notify them immediately. If your earnings will be higher, you may be overpaid and have to pay money back (overpayments are discussed in full in Chapter 11). If you will earn less, you may be delayed in receiving additional money due to you.

Sometimes, people report that they will not earn over the limit for the year, but then it turns out that they do. Many people think that they do not have to tell Social Security until they actually earn over the limit. This is incorrect and could result in an overpayment. You should notify Social Security at the time you expect your earnings to go over the limit, not when they actually do.

Except for annual reports of earnings (see Sec. 903), there are no formal requirements for notifying Social Security of an expected change in your earnings. You may call them on the phone, write a letter, or visit the District Office. If you write, address your letter to the attention of the "Service Unit" and include your claim number. (see Sec. 1407.) The letter should be mailed to your local District Office. (see Sec. 105.)

There are no penalties for not notifying Social Security about a change in your earnings estimate, but you must file an annual report for the year if your earnings are over the limit. You may be overpaid and have to pay money back if you delay telling Social Security about an increase in your earnings.

❏ Section 902.3 Annual Report of Earnings

If you receive Social Security benefits during a calendar year b but your earnings for that year were over the exempt amount, you are required by law to file an annual report of earnings, and you may be penalized if you do not. If you did not earn over the limit, you do not have to file an annual report. The earnings limitations are discussed in full in Chapter 8.

If you are entitled to benefits, but were not paid them, you should file an annual report even if your earnings are less than what you told Social Security. If you do not file an annual report in that case, you may not get those benefits for many years.

It is possible to have substantial earnings for a year and still be entitled to some Social Security benefits, especially if a wife is also entitled on the account.

The annual report must be filed no later than April 15 of the year following the year in question. If you are on a fiscal year basis, the annual report must be filed no later than three months and fifteen days after the end of your fiscal year.

Social Security regularly mails annual report forms to beneficiaries who received benefits during the year. However, you are responsible for filing the annual report even if you are not sent the form. The annual report may be filed with any district office, or mailed to the address on the form.

There are two annual report forms. One form asks for only two pieces of information: how much you earned in the year being reported, and how much you expect to earn in the current year. Benefits will be paid to you for the current year based on the estimate you put on the form. The other form asks an additional question about the amount of your monthly earnings for the year being reported.

As noted in Section 804, every beneficiary is entitled to one year during which the benefits may be paid for a month with earnings less than the monthly exempt amount, no matter how high the annual earnings are. You may only use this monthly earnings test during one calendar year. This is referred to as the *grace year*. If you have not used a grace year you will be sent the annual report form that asks about the monthly earnings.

Penalties may be imposed if you do not file the annual report on time. (see Sec. 903.)

Late Filing—Penalties

Section 903

If you do not file your annual report of earnings by the deadline (usually April 15 of the following year, see Sec. 903) you will be subject to penalties if you were overpaid during the year in question.

The amount of the penalty is equal to one month's benefit if this is the first time you have failed to file the annual report on time. If this is the second time, the penalty will be equal to two month's benefits. If it is the third time or more, the penalty will be three months' benefits. Social Security uses the benefit amount for December of the year involved for the penalty. If the amount of money overpaid for the year is less than the monthly benefit amount for the December benefit, the penalty will be equal to the amount you were overpaid.

For example, if you were overpaid only $100, the penalty will be $100, instead of the monthly benefit amount (minimum of $10) but only for the first time you fail to file an annual report. For a second or later failure, the normal penalty may be less if the amount of your overpayment could have been deducted from a lesser number of months' benefits. In that case the penalty will be equal to only the number of months that would have had deductions because of the earnings.

For example, a beneficiary with a monthly benefit rate of $400 per month has an overpayment of $600. This is the third time he has failed to file his annual report. The penalty for failure to file will be equal to only two months of benefits ($800) because the $600 overpayment would have caused deductions in only two months.

If you were paid the correct amount of benefits for the year being reported, or if money is due for the year being reported, there is no penalty for filing a late report of annual earnings.

If you can establish that you had good cause for not filing on time, there will be no penalty. Generally, good cause can be found only if you took all reasonable steps to comply with your responsibility, or if you were prevented from filing due to circumstances beyond your control, such as a physical or mental condition.

REPORTING CHANGES IN MARITAL STATUS

Section 904

If you receive spouse's, widow's, or child's benefits you must report any change in your marital status. If you become divorced from the worker, although you may be eligible to continue receiving benefits as a divorced wife, you must report the divorce anyway. If you were married to the worker for ten years and are at least sixty-two, you may still receive benefits. (see Sec. 204.3.)

If you receive benefits as a divorced wife or widow, you must report a remarriage. Divorced widows who re-marry after age sixty (or after age fifty if disabled) may continue to receive benefits, the same as non-divorced widows who remarry after age sixty. Widow's benefits will not be terminated due to remarriage if it occurs after age sixty. You should nevertheless report it for the record, to change your name and identification code. (see Sec. 1407.)

If a person who receives a child's benefit marries, the benefits usually terminate. This must be reported to Social Security.

If one Social Security beneficiary marries another, (depending on that types of beneficiaries) the benefits may not terminate, even though they would if the marriage was not occurring between beneficiaries. A chart that tells you whether or not benefits will terminate due to remarriage is located in Appendix 10.

If you receive child's benefits as a stepchild, you do not have to report the divorce of your natural parent and your stepparent. This will not affect your eligibility. Once a stepchild is entitled to benefits on the stepparent's account, the benefits will continue despite a divorce.

If you receive benefits only on your own account, you do not have to report any change in your marital status, unless you wish a name change.

REPORTING CHANGES IN STUDENT STATUS
Section 905

As noted in Sections 205.1 and in 409.1, in certain cases, a child may continue to receive child's benefits after age eighteen if that child is a full-time student. If you are receiving benefits on this basis, you must report any change in your full-time school status. If you are over age eighteen and are no longer a full time student, your benefits will terminate.

REPORTING CHILD NOT IN CARE
Section 906

If you receive spouse's or widow's benefits because you have a child in your care (see Sec. 207.8), your monthly benefit will be suspended for any month during which you do not have the child in your care. This does not terminate your benefits, it only suspends them. (see Sec. 1008.) You must report this to Social Security. Short absences of less than one month do not count. Only if the child is gone for the entire month must it be reported to Social Security.

If the child goes away on vacation, your benefits will not be suspended if you are still responsible for the child's upbringing and exercising parental control and supervision. However, if the child goes to live with another parent for more than one month, you must report because it will result in suspension of your benefits for that month.

A penalty may be imposed for failing to report not having a child in your care. The penalty amount is equal to the benefit amount for the first month of a period in which the child is not in your care. The penalty for a second failure is twice the benefit amount. The penalty for a third subsequent failure is three times the benefit amount. The penalty cannot exceed the amount of benefits which should have been suspended.

REPORTING DEATH

Section 907

The death of a Social Security beneficiary should be reported immediately. A check received after the death of a beneficiary cannot be cashed. It must be returned to the SSA. If you cash a check for a beneficiary who has died, you may be subject to criminal penalties. A benefit is not payable for the month of death. A check received after the death may be due for an earlier month; if so, it must be reissued by Social Security. It cannot be cashed. (see Sec. 1408.)

In the case of a husband and wife who receive a combined check, it should be brought to the local Social Security District Office. A service representative or a claim representative will stamp the back of the check with a special endorsement called a *superendorsement*, that will make it payable to the surviving beneficiary. You can then cash the check. Social Security will adjust your future benefits to take this into account.

Reporting Changes in Disability Cases

Section 908

People who receive benefits because they are disabled do not have to file an annual report of earnings, because the annual earnings limitations do not apply in disability cases. The earnings test does apply to spouses or children of disabled workers. Any work activity by a disabled beneficiary should be reported immediately to Social Security, regardless of the amount of earnings expected. The fact that you are working may have an effect on your continued eligibility to receive disability benefits. (see Sec. 504.)

If you receive benefits because of disability, you should report any medical improvement in your condition, because you may no longer be totally disabled. There is no penalty for failure to report a medical improvement.

Reporting Work Outside the U.S.

Section 909

You must report to Social Security as soon as you have worked seven or more days in one month in a foreign country. (see Sec. 811.) You are subject to a penalty for failing to report in the same way that penalties are imposed for failing to report that a child is not in your care. (see Sec. 906.)

PAYMENT, NON-PAYMENT, AND NON-RECEIPT OF CHECKS

10

CHECKS IN GENERAL

Section 1001

Social Security benefits are issued by the Treasury Department on regular green government checks. The check will have the Social Security number of the worker on whose account the benefits are based and will also have the beneficiary identification code, which indicates which type of benefit you are receiving. (see Sec. 1407.) The checks can be mailed to your home, to your post office box, or directly to your bank. (see Sec. 1006.)

Social Security benefits are not assignable, and are not subject to attachment or levy by creditors. You can have them sent in care of someone else for mailing purposes, but Social Security will want an explanation. They will want to make sure that no one else is depriving you of your Social Security benefits.

THE FIRST CHECK

Section 1002

When you apply for Social Security benefits, you may be required to submit certain documents. (see Chapter 4.) After you have submitted everything required, you should receive your first check in about one month. This is the average processing time. Sometimes it takes as little as ten to fifteen days; sometimes it can take up to three months. It is rare, but occasionally it can take more than three months before the first check is sent out. Of course, the check will not be paid until it is due.

If you apply in advance of the time you are first eligible for benefits, you will not receive a check until you meet the eligibility requirement. For instance, if you apply for retirement benefits three months before you turn sixty-two, you will not receive the check until after your birthday. Remember that checks are paid in arrears. (see Sec. 1003.)

If you have applied for Social Security benefits after the first month in which you are entitled, the first check may include retroactive benefits due for the past period. There is a full discussion of applications and retroactivity in Chapter 4.

Social Security has different procedures and systems for processing cases. Some cases can go through a computer system, other cases cannot. The cases that can go through the computer are processed much more quickly than the others.

About a month after you apply for benefits, you can call the local district office to find out when you may expect to receive the first check. They usually will not be able to tell you how long it will take until approximately four weeks after you apply. They will be able to tell you at that time whether you can expect payment within a few weeks or a few more months.

REGULAR MONTHLY CHECKS

Section 1003

After you have become entitled to Social Security benefits you will receive your checks on a monthly basis. The checks are paid one month in arrears. This means for example, that the check you receive in May is the benefit due for the month of April. For beneficiaries entitled before May 1997, the check is paid on the third day of the month unless the third is a Saturday, Sunday or a holiday, in which case it will be paid before the third. For beneficiaries entitled beginning May, 1997 the checks payment days are staggered according to birthday.

If your birthday is the on the first through the tenth day of the month, you receive your check on the second Wednesday of the month; for those born on the eleventh through the twentieth, the check comes on the third Wednesday, and for those born on the twenty-first through the thirty-first, it comes on the fourth Wednesday.

Always remember that the check you receive on the third of the month is the benefit due for the preceding month; benefits are paid in arrears.

COMBINED CHECKS

Section 1004

If two or more people who live in the same household receive benefits on the same account, the Social Security Administration (SSA) will usually combine the payments for each beneficiary into one monthly check (but not a parent and child). For example, if a husband and wife are both receiving benefits on the husband's account, they will get one monthly check, which will have both of their names on it.

If the wife has worked on her own record and is entitled to benefits on her own account in addition to the wife's benefits, the checks will not be combined; each person will receive his or her own check. If you do not want your benefits combined into one check, you may request that they be issued separately.

If you receive combined payments in one check, and then one beneficiary dies, the surviving beneficiary can take the check to the local Social Security district office to have it made payable to him or her. The amount of benefits will be adjusted at a later time, although this may take several months.

SPECIAL CHECKS

Section 1005

Once you are receiving your regular monthly checks, you may be due an increase for different reasons. (see Sec. 704.) If Social Security increases your benefit amount after the time you are first entitled to the increase, you will receive the increases for each unpaid month retroactively in one check.

For example, let us say that you were working even after you first became eligible for Social Security benefits. Your earnings may increase your benefit amount. (see Sec. 704.3.)

Social Security will automatically recompute your benefit, but it may take them years to do it. If you have earnings in a year after the year that you become eligible for benefits, your new earnings may cause an increase in your benefit amount beginning with the January of the first year after the year of the new earnings. You may request a re-calculation as soon as you get your W-2, or you may wait for them to do so automatically. Sometimes, it may take Social Security years to make the re-calculation, but when they do, they will pay the past-due increases in a lump sum.

This check will be in an odd amount and can arrive at any time during the month, or the money can be combined with a regular check. You will usually receive a letter explaining why you are receiving the check or the odd payment, but the letter may come after you receive the check. It should come within about two weeks either before or after. If you receive an odd check and you do not receive an explanation letter within two weeks, contact your Social Security office.

DIRECT DEPOSIT

Section 1006

If you wish, you can have your Social Security checks sent directly to your bank instead of to your home. This can be very convenient, for obvious reasons. You must be receiving regular monthly checks. To arrange for this you must contact your bank, not the District Office. The bank must fill out certain forms, and they will notify Social Security. It may take up to three months. If it does not start within that time, get a copy of the form from the bank and bring it to the District Office. They can make the computer inputs from the copy.

Non-Payment in General

Section 1007

Regular monthly checks will stop if Social Security determines that your eligibility has terminated (see Sec. 1009) or that you are subject to suspension. (see Sec. 1008.) Before the benefits actually stop, you should receive notice of Social Security's intention to terminate or suspend your benefits. You generally have a right to appeal these decisions. (see Chapter 13.)

Sometimes you may receive only a partial benefit for the month. If you must pay back money because you have been overpaid, you may arrange for deductions from your monthly benefits over a period of time, instead of withholding the full benefit amount until the overpayment is recovered.

If you are due a check for a month but you do not receive it, you should follow the guidelines in Section 1011.

Suspension of Benefits

Section 1008

In some cases, even though you remain legally entitled to benefits, the payment may be suspended. The most common example of this is when benefits are suspended because of earnings. There is a full discussion of the Work Test in Chapter 8.

If you are a young wife or a young widow (eligibility based on having a child in your care), you are subject to a suspension of benefits for any full month during which you do not have a child who is entitled to benefits on the same account "in your care." Temporary absences do not count.

If your child is away on vacation with relatives or at a boarding school, you are considered to have a child in your care if you are exercising parental control and responsibility over the child. If you are separated from the other parent, you are subject to suspension for any month during which the child is with that parent.

Social Security looks at the calendar months involved, and not the total number of days. If the child is in your care for at least one day during a calendar month, the benefit will not be suspended.

Another common reason for suspension of benefits is in the case of a spouse or a widow(er) who is eligible for a governmental pension based on his or her own earnings. (see Sec. 705.4.) Before July 1983, there is a dollar for dollar offset. If the governmental pension is greater than the Social Security benefit, no Social Security benefit is payable. Beginning with July 1983, only two-thirds of the governmental pension offsets Social Security benefits.

If your benefits are in suspense, you are still legally entitled, although you will not receive the benefit for any suspense month. Once the event causing suspense stops, your benefits can be resumed without the need for another application. You will notify Social Security of the change, and the benefits will be started again.

TERMINATION OF BENEFITS

Section 1009

In Chapter 2, each type of Social Security benefit is specifically described, including the events that will terminate benefits.

Benefits terminate upon death, and sometimes they will terminate upon divorce or marriage. Disability benefits may terminate if there is a medical recovery or if you return to work.

Whatever the cause, benefits terminate the month before the month of the occurrence of the terminating event. For instance, in the case of death, if a beneficiary dies in the month of August, the benefits terminate with the month of July. This sounds strange, but it really is not. Remember that checks are paid in arrears so that the payment received in August is actually the payment for July.

In all cases except disability (see Sec. 513), the benefit is payable for the month of termination, so that although the benefits terminate the month before the month of the event, the check is payable for the terminating month. In the case of the beneficiary who dies in August, the August 3 check, which is payable for the month of July, is due and payable. The September 3 check, which would otherwise be due for the month of August, is not payable and must be returned.

These rules apply to all types of events causing termination of benefits, including death, marriage, remarriage, etc. Disability benefits may stop because you return to work or because you make a medical recovery. In these cases, the termination of benefits occurs two months after the month the disability ceases.

For example, if your disability ceases because of a medical improvement in June, the termination applies to the month of August. Benefits are payable for the month of June, July, and August, but not after August because that is the month of termination.

If you appeal a decision to terminate your disability benefits, you may request your benefits to continue until you receive a hearing. (see Sec. 1305.) If you have had a hearing but your case is still under appeal, it must be re-evaluated. If you lose after the hearing, the benefits will be considered an overpayment. However, if you have made the request in good faith, you may qualify for waiver. (see Chapter 11.)

LOST OR STOLEN CHECKS

Section 1010

If your monthly check has been lost or stolen you should report this immediately to the Social Security office. They will issue a stop payment on that check and will reissue a replacement check. Usually you will receive the replacement within fifteen days.

If you find the lost or stolen check, before the replacement check is issued, you can cash the check but you must notify Social Security that you found it. If you receive the replacement check anyway it must be returned.

When Social Security puts a stop payment on a check, it takes a long time for it to become effective. If you find your missing check within a week or two after you have reported it as lost or stolen, you should be able to cash it.

A replacement check will have your Social Security claim number (see Sec. 1407) on it and will say that it is a substitute check. It will not be dated the third day of the month. It will be dated as of the date that it is actually issued.

If the check is not lost or stolen but is only misplaced, Social Security will not make an immediate reissue. They will wait three days after it was issued. Action is taken to immediately replace a lost or stolen check. If your check is stolen or lost you must be able to give some reason why you believe it is stolen or lost rather than temporarily misplaced.

WHAT TO DO IF YOUR CHECK DOES NOT COME

Section 1011

The overwhelming majority of the beneficiaries receive their Social Security checks on time each month without experiencing any delays or interruptions, but sometimes there are problems. Each month there are thousands of people across the country who do not receive their checks when they should.

As noted in Section 1002, the first check after you apply for benefits can take anywhere from two weeks to three months and sometimes more. If you do not receive the first check within a month of the date that it is due, you should call your Social Security office to find out whether you can expect it in the near future, or whether it will take several more months. Some cases can be processed through the computer system and other cases cannot. The cases that go through the computer system are done faster.

If your case is not being handled this way, Social Security will tell you. Expect an additional two to three months for your check to come. If Social Security tells you that the check will come within two months, do not call them back the next week and ask where it is. Sometimes you can actually delay the processing of your claim by making too many inquiries.

If you have not received your first check within ninety days of the time that you gave Social Security all the information and documents they requested, you have a right to an expedited payment. This is discussed in Section 1013.

After your initial claim is processed your case will be set up on the computer system so that you will receive regular monthly checks automatically. Checks are usually paid on the third day of the month. If your check is received, but is lost or stolen, see Sec. 1010. In that case you should notify Social Security immediately. If your check is not received at all, you should wait three mailing days before notifying Social Security. Sometimes delays occur with the Post Office.

If your check does not come when it should, there is no point notifying Social Security before three mailing days have passed. First of all, the Social Security telephone lines and the Social Security district office will be jammed with other people who have not received their checks on time. It will take you a long time to get through to somebody at Social Security in the beginning of the month for this reason. But the most important reason for not notifying Social Security until three mailing days have passed is because Social Security will not do anything before then anyway.

Their procedures require them to wait three mailing days before taking any action to replace the check. If you should finally get through to a district office before the third mailing day after the check is due, they will simply send you a form to complete and mail back to them.

If you have not received the check by the third mailing day, steps will be taken to issue a replacement. If your check does not come on the third, do not get upset. In most cases you will receive it within three mailing days. If you do not receive it after that, you should notify Social Security of the non-receipt of the check. A sample form is located in Appendix 9.

This form can be used to notify Social Security of your missing check. Otherwise you can visit the district office in person, call, or write a letter. The easiest way is to write a letter, because the phones and offices will be very busy during the first week of any given month.

If you write a letter, you should include certain basic information. Give your complete name, your correct mailing address, and your former mailing address if you have had a recent change. You must also indicate the claim number and your beneficiary identification code. (see Sec. 1407.)

Your notice of non-receipt of a check should identify which monthly check has not been received. You can do this by indicating the day the check was due, such as the September 3 check, or you can describe it as the month for which the check is payable. For instance, the September 3 check is payable for the August benefit. To avoid confusion, you should indicate the month for which the benefit is payable as well as the date you expected the payment. For example, you should say that it is the September 3 check for the August benefit.

If your checks are directly deposited to your bank account, do not contact Social Security at all. The bank must send paperwork to notify Social Security. If you contact Social Security instead of the bank, they will tell you to contact the bank because a bank officer must sign a form before Social Security can do anything.

When you mail a notice of non-receipt of a check, address it to your local district office, attention "Service Unit." The Service Unit in the district office handles non-receipt notice. (see Sec. 105.)

After you have sent your notice of non-receipt, give it about a week and then call to see if it was received. It will be easier at that time to get through to the district office, and they should be able to tell you whether they have your notice. It takes about fifteen days after the notice of non-receipt is processed by the district office for a replacement check to be issued.

If you have not received a check within fifteen days, you should again contact the Social Security district office. They will tell you when to expect the check. It is important not to call them before the time frames they give you. If you call too soon the case may have to be pulled out of its normal processing to answer your question. This can result in even further delay.

If you have not received a regular monthly check within a month and a half after it was due, you have a right to an expedited payment. (see Sec. 1013.)

REPLACEMENT CHECKS

Section 1012

If you notify Social Security that your check is lost or stolen or that you did not receive it (see Secs. 1010 and 1011), you will be sent a replacement check. This will be a special check that may arrive at any time of the month and may be dated as of any date.

Of course, you cannot keep both your regular check and the replacement check. If you end up receiving both, one or the other must be returned. It does not matter which one is returned. You can cash whichever one you receive first. If you keep both checks you will be overpaid and will be required to make a refund. In these cases you are almost never eligible for waiver of repayment.

EXPEDITED PAYMENTS

Section 1013

The Social Security Act puts certain deadlines on the time when checks must be paid to you by Social Security. The rules are different depending on whether it is your first check or a regular monthly payment.

In a case involving your first check after you apply for benefits, you may request an expedited payment if the check has not been paid to you within ninety days of the time you gave all the evidence requested by Social Security to support the claim (except in disability cases). Social Security is then required by law to pay you within fifteen days of your request.

To file the request, you should go to your district office and tell them you want the expedited payment. If preferred, you may send a letter. The request must be in writing; you cannot make it over the phone. If you go to the district office, they will prepare a written request for you. If you file your request before ninety days have passed, Social Security will not act on it until the end of the ninety-day period.

Please note that if you file your application for benefits before the month you are entitled to payment, the ninety days will run from the date on which the first payment is due, not from the date you submit your last evidence. For example, if you file in June for benefits beginning with the month of September, the ninety-day period begins running from October 3. (October 3 is the payment check for the September benefits.)

If you are receiving regular monthly benefits, a request for expedited payment may be filed thirty days after the fifteenth day of the month in which the payment was due. For example, if you are receiving regular monthly benefits on the third of each month and you do not receive the check due on September third, you may request an expedited payment if you have not received it within thirty days of September 15. The payment must then be issued to you within fifteen days of that request. The request for expedited payment can be filed earlier, but it will not be acted upon until after the thirty days runs out.

If you do not receive your check despite your request for expedited payment, and you are not satisfied with the explanations you are getting from Social Security, you may wish to contact an elected official. (see Sec. 1014.)

WHEN TO GO TO YOUR CONGRESSMAN

Section 1014

Sometimes, even with the best efforts of Social Security employees, problems can occur that delay payments. If you have followed the procedures outlined in the above sections, but still have not received your check, an elected official will help push your case. You should contact your United States Congressman or your United States Senator. Each Congressman's office usually has a person who keeps in touch with SSA.

When the Social Security office receives an inquiry from a Congressman, they will take steps to make sure that your case is handled as quickly as possible. Social Security will locate your folder and put a special "flag" on it to indicate that there is a Congressional inquiry. This will make sure that the case does not get lost in the shuffle, and regular reports will be made to the manager of the Social Security office, who in turn will make reports to the Congressman's office.

It is important to contact your Congressman only when all else fails. If you contact your Congressman too soon it may result in additional delays on your case. This is because the case may have to be pulled out of its normal processing to answer the Congressman's inquiry. Call your Congressman only after you have followed the guidelines in the above sections.

OVERPAYMENTS 11

OVERPAYMENTS IN GENERAL

Section 1101

An overpayment arises when you get more Social Security benefits than you are legally entitled to receive. Each year thousands of people are overpaid benefits. Overpayments occur for many reasons. Sometimes it is Social Security's fault, sometimes it is the beneficiary's fault, and sometimes it is a combination of both. Of course, Social Security would like to recover any benefits that are erroneously paid. A major effort is now being undertaken by the Social Security Administration (SSA) to collect back as much of these overpaid benefits as possible.

However, the law and the Social Security rules allow for "waiver" of repayment of the overpayment. In certain cases, a beneficiary who has been overpaid will not be required to make a refund. This chapter will discuss the rules and guidelines Social Security uses when determining whether to require a full refund of an overpayment.

COMMON CAUSES OF OVERPAYMENT

Section 1102

There are two separate categories of overpayments. The most usual one is called a *deduction overpayment*. In these cases, the beneficiary is legally entitled to benefits, but for some other reason part or all of the benefits should not have been paid. This situation frequently arises when the beneficiary has earnings over the limit for the year, but benefits have been paid based on a lower estimate.

Another common cause of overpayments is when a new beneficiary becomes entitled on the same Social Security account. For example, a man dies, leaving his wife and two children. They become entitled to benefits. Several months later, a child by a previous marriage applies for benefits on that account. Because of the family maximum provisions (see Sec. 703.2), an overpayment arises retroactively.

When there are three or more beneficiaries receiving survivor benefits, the family maximum is usually met. When the widow and first two children filed and started receiving benefits, they were paid on the assumption that there would be only three beneficiaries on the account. When the child from the first marriage applies, his application can be retroactive for up to six months. Although the benefits will be refigured for the future and the first two children and widow will receive less, the benefits for the past are now higher than they should have been.

Another type of overpayment is called an *entitlement overpayment*. This occurs when you file for benefits and Social

Security pays them but later discovers that you were never eligible. Any benefits you received are an overpayment.

Sometimes overpayments can occur due to clerical errors. When your benefits are calculated, they are based on the amount of the earnings. Sometimes a clerical error can occur so that the amount of your earnings is figured at a higher level, than it should be. This means that the amount of your benefit has been greater than it should be, and the difference is an overpayment.

OVERPAYMENT PROCEDURES

Section 1103

Once Social Security determines that a person has been overpaid, a decision must be made about whether to collect back the overpayment or to waive it. If waived, Social Security will not require repayment. Social Security's guidelines and procedures for waiver of repayment are discussed in Sections 1104-1109.

If Social Security requires a refund, this can be done in different ways. They may accept a partial refund as a compromise in full settlement (see Secs. 1110-1111) or allow for repayment over a period of time. (see Secs. 1113-1114.)

When Social Security determines that you have been overpaid a letter will be sent to you advising you of that fact and of the amount of the overpayment. The letter will explain how the overpayment occurred. Social Security will always request a full refund of the overpaid amount.

If you do not agree that there has been an overpayment or with the amount of the overpayment, you may request a reconsideration. (see Chapter 13.)

In the overpayment letter Social Security says they will start withholding one hundred percent of your monthly benefits until the full amount of overpayment has been recovered. If you request an appeal, a waiver, or some other method of repayment, Social Security will hold up any further processing of the recovery until a decision has been made on your request.

WAIVER OF OVERPAYMENT

Section 1104

Social Security will not require you to refund an overpayment if certain conditions are met. To be eligible you must be *without fault* in causing the overpayment (see Sec. 1105), and repayment would either be *against equity and good conscience,* or it would *defeat the purpose of Title II of the Social Security Act.*

There are two requirements for waiver of repayment. The first is without fault, and the second is alternative: either "against equity and good conscience" or "defeat the purpose of Title II." Without fault is discussed in Section 1105; against equity and good conscience is discussed in Section 1106; and defeat the purpose of Title II is discussed in Section 1107.

You must satisfy the *without fault* requirement in all cases, and either one of the two alternative requirements. An overpayment may be waived if you are without fault and recovery would be against equity and good conscience, or if you are without fault and recovery would defeat the purpose of Title II.

The purpose of Title II of the Social Security Act is to provide a minimum income for persons who are deprived of income by reason of retirement, death, or disability. This requirement may be met if recovery of the over payment will prevent you from meeting your ordinary and necessary living expenses and you have insufficient assets.

If you are found eligible for waiver, you will not be required to repay the overpayment. The slate will be wiped clean and you will have no obligation for repayment at any time.

If you are not eligible for waiver, you will be required to repay. This can be done by a compromise settlement in a lesser sum (see Secs. 1110-1111), by partial payments (see Sec. 1114) or by deductions from your checks. (see Sec. 1113.)

"WITHOUT FAULT"

Section 1105

Generally, *without fault* means that you gave all information that was necessary to determine your benefits to SSA and that you could not reasonably be expected to know that an over-payment would occur by accepting and cashing a particular check. If you cannot establish that you were without fault in causing an overpayment, the recovery of the overpayment can never be waived. Without fault is a requirement which must be met in all cases of waiver.

SSA may have been at fault in causing the overpayment; nevertheless, you must establish that you were without fault. SSA's fault does not excuse yours.

Each particular case will be examined to determine its own specific facts. The general principles are that the beneficiary must report everything that may affect payment of benefits, and must exercise a high degree of care when determining whether a check is payable.

There are many situations that have occurred repeatedly involving the question of whether or not a beneficiary was at fault in causing an overpayment. SSA has identified certain situations in which it is presumed that the beneficiary is without fault in the absence of other information to indicate otherwise. These situations are described in Section 1105.

There are some situations in which SSA presumes the beneficiary is at fault. The most obvious case is when duplicate payments have been made. If you cash your regular monthly check as well as a replacement check, you will not be considered without fault. If you file an application for benefits but you are already receiving on another account, you are at fault if you accept benefits from both accounts, unless you have told SSA that you are already entitled on the first account.

You are at fault in causing an overpayment if you do not exercise a high degree of care about your monthly benefits. If, for example, you return to work but do not report it, you will be at fault if an overpayment results.

If you do not deal in good faith, you will not be held to be without fault. For example, if you incurred an overpayment in one year because of work, requested and obtained a waiver of repayment, but then worked again in the following year, you will not be considered without fault for the second year because you knew that your earnings would affect your benefits.

If you withhold information from SSA that could affect your benefits, you will not be without fault. At the time you file your application, you are given a receipt that lists the things that must be reported. From time to time, SSA puts "stuffers" into check envelopes to remind you of things to report.

Examples of Without Fault

Over the years SSA has become aware of certain typical situations in which the overpaid person is without fault. They have identified these situations and will assume, if your case fits within these facts, that you are without fault in causing the overpayment. This assumption may be overcome by other facts that show bad faith or failure to exercise a high degree of care about your monthly benefits.

Situation One: A person is usually found to be without fault if there is a mistake about the benefit rates. SSA will not require you to know the exact amount of your monthly benefits, but if the error is so grossly disproportionate to what your payment should be, you may be at fault.

Example: John applied for retirement benefits and was told he would receive $600 per month. The first check was for $600, but the second check was for $6,000. This payment is so out of line with what he should have expected, that he may be at fault unless he has attempted to verify it with SSA.

If he received checks in the amount of $620 all along after he retired and then was advised a year later that the correct amount should have been only $600,

Social Security will consider him to be without fault in causing the overpayment, because he cannot be expected to calculate the exact benefit amount.

Situation Two: If you file for monthly benefits and you are told that you have earned enough to be eligible, but it later turns out you have not, you will be considered without fault in causing any overpayment (unless your earnings record was fraudulent).

Situation Three: If you believed that only the net amount of your paycheck counted towards the retirement test, you may be considered without fault in causing an overpayment. If your earnings for a year are above a certain level, this will cause a reduction in your benefits. The gross amount of earnings, before taxes are deducted, is what counts.

Many times, a beneficiary believes that only his take home pay is counted for the annual earnings limitation or the monthly limit. Your "take home" pay is the amount of your paycheck after all deductions, such as income tax, union dues, insurance, hospitalization, etc. If your net cash earnings (take home pay) for the year is below the annual earnings limit, then Social Security will generally consider you to be "without fault" if you believed that only your take home pay counted. If your net cash earnings is over the limit for the year, SSA will consider whether or not you reported the net amount or the gross amount for purposes of the annual earnings limitations.

If you report the amount of take home pay to SSA this will indicate that you understood that only the take home pay counted and not the gross pay. Social Security will want to look at your pay stubs to determine the net amount of your take home pay. If you cannot obtain them, they will usually contact your employer to find this out.

Situation Four: You will be considered to be without fault in causing an overpayment if you relied on incorrect information from an official source. An *official source* means SSA or another government agency which you reasonably thought was connected with the administration of social security, such as the Railroad Retirement Board. Misunderstanding of correctly given information does not count as misinformation for these purposes.

If you claim misinformation was given to you, Social Security will question you very closely to determine whether you misunderstood correct information or whether misinformation was, in fact, given. They will look to determine your normal understanding, because some people can understand technical requirements better than others.

You must give a full explanation of your reliance on wrong information. They will ask for an explanation in your own words. The explanation will have to show what information was received, the time and place it was received, the identity (if possible) of the person who gave the incorrect information, and any and all other facts about the situation.

SSA will seek to verify the statements you give by contacting the people within the district office or elsewhere who you say gave you the misinformation. If supporting evidence cannot be obtained, the manager or supervisor in the office will make a report as to the likelihood of misinformation being given. If records are no longer available and there is no way to verify your allegations, they will resolve the doubt about it in your favor.

Situation Five: If an overpayment results because a short taxable year for the beneficiary is caused by his death, Social Security will waive any overpayment if there is evidence that the deceased beneficiary intended to limit his yearly earnings to the annual earnings limitations in effect for the year of death. If he dies before December of the year, the annual earnings limit is prorated according to the number of months the beneficiary was alive. (see Sec. 810.)

For example, if the beneficiary died in the month of June the earnings limitation would be half of the annual limit for the year. If the beneficiary had earned less than the annual limit up to the time he died and did not intend to earn over the regular limit for the year, the overpayment resulting from the excess earnings will usually be waived. Recovery in this case is deemed to be against equity and good conscience.

Situation Six: Sometimes, a person is overpaid because he has earned more than the allowable earnings limit for a particular year, without realizing that his earnings before he became entitled to benefits in that year would count.

For example, you start receiving benefits in June. Your earnings for June through December are only $3,000, well below the annual earnings limit. But you also worked from January through May and earned $10,000. The total yearly earnings are $13,000 and will cause deductions for any month in which you have earned over the monthly limit. (see Sec. 804.)

If you have received all your monthly benefits and have earned over the monthly limit in all months, you have been overpaid. If you believed that your earnings before you became entitled to benefits did not count for the earnings test, Social Security will consider you to be without fault in causing the overpayment. For this rule to apply, your earnings for the year beginning with the time you become eligible must not exceed the annual earnings limit for that year.

The intent of this rule is to provide for a "without fault" finding if you restrict your earnings to the yearly limit, beginning with the time you become eligible for benefits. Although all of your earnings for the year are included for purposes of the work test, if you were unaware of this and believed in good faith that only your earnings after entitlement counted, Social Security may find you to be without fault.

If you are an employee and your wages in the deduction months (months which are subject to withholding because of earnings) did not exceed the total monthly benefit for that month, recovery of the overpayment is deemed inequitable. In this situation the overpayment may be waived without considering your financial circumstances. The following example shows the application of these rules.

Example: William began his entitlement to retirement benefits in March 2001. His monthly amount was established at $900. He earned $4,000 in January and February. His wife also became entitled to wife's benefits in the amount of $450. Benefit checks were issued to Mr. Smith and his wife each month beginning with March 2001, based on his statement that he would not earn over the yearly amount permitted under the law. Mr. Smith's employer later reported wages of $15,160 in 2001. It seems that Mr. Smith misunderstood the retirement test. Mr. Smith believed that he could earn $10,680 after qualifying for benefits and reduced his hours of work so his earnings would not exceed $10,680 ($1,068 per month for ten months).

On the basis of his earnings, he and his wife were overpaid. Mr. Smith is without fault in incurring the overpayment, and recovery is deemed to be against equity and good conscience because the earnings in each of the months affected by the potential deductions (March and April) are less than his monthly benefit amount for those months.

The term *eligibility* for benefits is used broadly for purposes of this rule. It does not necessarily mean legal entitlement. It usually means what the beneficiary understands. If the beneficiary believes that his earnings before he files his application do not count, Social Security looks at it from that view. If he believes that his earnings before reaching retirement age will not count, they will apply the rule that way.

Situation Seven: If your earnings for a year are more than you expected them to be, you may be found to be without fault in causing a resulting overpayment if the reason the earnings are greater is one of the following:

- you received a retroactive increase in pay;

- your rate of pay was higher than you realized;

- you made an agreement with your employer that your earnings would be kept below a certain limit, but the employer did not restrict the earnings and you were unable to keep accurate records; or

- there were five pay days in a month and you only expected four pay days, (if your monthly earnings with only four pay days would be under the monthly limit), or you figured your annual earnings based on four pay days per month and you would have been under the yearly limit on that basis.

Situation Eight: You may be without fault in causing an overpayment if Social Security continued to send you checks after you notified them of your return to work, or of something else that should have caused a deduction. You qualify under this rule if you believe in good faith that you are entitled to receive the checks because Social Security is still sending them to you. SSA will want to know how and when you gave notice of the events that were reported, and what your reaction was to the continued payment of monthly checks.

Many times, a person will say that notice of the deduction event (such as return to work or not having a child in your care) was supposed to be given by a relative or friend. If this is the case, Social Security will not consider you without fault because you have the duty to report these events, not someone else. However, if you routinely rely on this other person to report these things for you, Social Security may take that as a circumstance to consider. For instance, if you are housebound or unable to speak English and your daughter or son takes care of your affairs, Social Security may allow that as a reasonable excuse.

Situation Nine: Sometimes, overpayments occur because employees receive special types of payments that they do not realize are included in annual earnings for purposes of the retirement test. If you believe in good faith that a bonus, vacation pay, traveling expense, or other similar payment was not to be included in figuring your earnings, Social Security may consider you to be without fault in causing an overpayment by the inclusion of those payments.

Social Security will contact your employer to determine the amount and the type of special payment involved. If you were unaware that those special payments counted, Social Security will generally consider you to be without fault in causing an overpayment resulting from that extra pay. Please note that you must still satisfy the second part of the waiver test. (see Sec. 1104.)

Situation Ten: Another common situation causing overpayments is when the beneficiary is confused with regard to how the annual earnings test works. An overpaid beneficiary sometimes believes that earnings over the limit for the taxable year cause deductions from checks only for months beginning with the first month in which earnings go over. If you report quickly to Social Security that your earnings have reached that level when they do, you may be eligible for a waiver if you are overpaid.

Two important factors are considered: 1) whether you, in fact, notified SSA when your earnings reached the yearly amount or immediately thereafter, and 2) if you did, waiver can apply only for months before the time you reported your earnings. You know that your earnings after you go over the limit will affect your benefit, so you cannot be without fault if you accept them.

Situation Eleven: If you receive benefits as a dependent on the account of a retired worker, your benefits may be subject to deductions if the worker earns over the annual limit. (see Sec. 801.) If you are overpaid as a result, you may be "without fault" if you did not know (and had no reason to know) that the worker's earnings would go over the limit, and you were not living with the worker. You must still meet the second part of the waiver rules. (see Sec. 1104.)

Situation Twelve: If your benefits end during a year, your earnings after termination nevertheless are counted for the work test. This may result in overpayment of benefits which were paid. If you believed that your earnings after termination of entitlement would not cause deductions for the earlier months, you may be without fault in causing the overpayment. You must still meet the second part of the waiver rules. (see Sec. 1104.)

Social Security will require a breakdown of your earnings to see if you earned over the yearly limit during the time you were entitled. They will require evidence of the earnings, such as pay stubs or a letter from your employer.

Situation Thirteen: You may be without fault in causing an overpayment if you made a good faith effort to restrict your earnings, but you misunderstood the retirement test or there was some other unusual circumstance.

Examples:

- A self-employed person believed the monthly wage limits applied instead of the "substantial services" rule. (see Sec. 804.)

- You wanted to restrict your earnings and kept an ongoing record, but you made an arithmetical error, or you lost a pay slip.

- You believed that you could earn up to the yearly limit beginning with the month of your first check up until the end of the year.

- You believed you could earn the yearly limit for a twelve month period that began with your first month of eligibility, for example March 1, 1994 through March 1, 1995, rather than a calendar year.

Social Security will require verification of what you say, such as evidence of your wages for specific periods.

"AGAINST EQUITY AND GOOD CONSCIENCE"

Section 1106

One of the alternatives of the second part of the waiver rules (see Sec. 1104) is that recovery of the overpayment (making you pay it back) would be against equity and good conscience. This occurs if, relying on payment of benefits, you gave up a valuable right, or changed your position for the worse. If you claim waiver because of this, Social Security will require you to give a full explanation of the circumstances. They will require verification of what you say. The evidence required will depend on the facts of your particular case (see the next section for some examples).

Remember that in all cases you must establish "without fault." (see Sec. 1105.) If you cannot establish "against equity and good conscience," you may still be eligible for waiver if you can establish that recovery would "defeat the purpose of Title II." (see Sec. 1107.)

EXAMPLES OF "AGAINST EQUITY AND GOOD CONSCIENCE"

Whether your case will be considered to meet the "against equity" requirement depends on the particular facts. Here are some examples of situations in which the requirement is satisfied.

Example 1: John applied for retirement benefits and was awarded. He resigned from his job, relying on the monthly benefits. Three years later it is discovered that his earnings record was wrong, without fault on John's part. He does not have the required insured status (see Sec. 601) and therefore he has been overpaid. Because of his age, he cannot get another job. Recovery of the overpayment would be against equity and good conscience.

Example 2: Agnes is a widow who applies for and receives survivor benefits. Counting on this income, she enters her daughter in college, which would not otherwise be possible. It turns out that her husband did not work long enough, and Agnes is therefore overpaid. Recovery of the overpayment would be inequitable.

OTHER SITUATIONS

In certain situations, you are considered to be without fault in causing an overpayment. (see Sec. 1105.) In some of these same cases, recovery is also considered to be against equity and good conscience, and you are therefore eligible for waiver of the overpayment. If so, you do not have to establish financial hardship.

Certain without fault situations are described in Section 1105. Situations three, four, and five of that section are also considered to meet the against equity rule. Situation six also meets the rule if you are an employee and your wages in months subject to deductions are less than the total monthly benefits for those months. This is discussed more fully in Section 1105, SITUATION SIX.

"DEFEAT THE PURPOSE OF TITLE II"

Section 1107

An alternative requirement of the second part of the waiver rules (see Sec. 1104) is that recovery of overpayment would *defeat the purpose of Title II of the Social Security Act.* This is the law that provides for social security benefits. Its purpose is to keep the disabled, the retired, and survivors out of destitution. You meet the *defeat the purpose* requirement if recovery of the overpayment would deprive you of funds necessary for your support.

Social Security looks first at your income (from all sources) and your ordinary and necessary living expenses. (see Sec. 1109.) If you do not need all of your income, then Social Security will look at your assets. If they are below certain levels, you will not have to repay the overpayment. (see Sec. 1108.)

If you do not meet the defeat the purpose requirement, you may be eligible for waiver if recovery would be against equity and good conscience. (see Sec. 1106.) In all cases, you must also be without fault for waiver to be approved. (see Sec. 1104.)

EXAMPLES OF "DEFEAT THE PURPOSES OF TITLE II"

Example 1: Virginia was overpaid $900. She had income of $195 from a private pension and $430 in Social Security benefits. She lived alone and had no dependents. Virginia listed current monthly expenses of $620, which included $275 rent for her apartment, $20 for clothes, $200 for food, $30 for medical care and prescriptions, $10 for church contributions, $30 for utilities, and $55 for auto maintenance and insurance.

She submitted bills verifying her rent, utilities, prescriptions, and automobile insurance. Since the overall expenses appeared reasonable and necessary for ordinary living expenses, a finding of defeat the purpose of Title II would be justified.

Example 2: Dan was overpaid $350.00. He and his wife live in a small home valued at $50,000. They also own a motor boat valued at $7,000 on which they still owe $4,000. Their only income is Social Security benefits of $600. They only have $200 in a savings account.

They state that their monthly expenses are $640 including $100 for property taxes, $300 for food, $20 for clothing, $20 for prescriptions, $50 for utilities, $50 for insurance and upkeep of their car, and $100 to repay the loan and to maintain their boat. As the boat is not a necessity and their expenses for ordinary living costs do not approach their income, a finding of defeat the purpose of Title II would not be justified.

Example 3: Will, his wife Mae, and his son Joe have $500 in the bank. Will lives in a low income housing project and alleges that his total monthly expenses are only $400, consisting of rent of $80, food of $300, and telephone of $20. His income is only $380. His expenses can be presumed to be reasonable. A finding of defeat the purpose of Title II would be justified. If, however, his monthly income were $450, defeat the purpose of Title II would not be justified.

Example 4: Joe was overpaid $600 because it was determined that he did not have enough work to collect Social Security benefits. He has no monthly income. He does have $5,000 in the bank. He has outstanding medical bills of $2,200, and more medical bills are coming in monthly. The medical bills will soon wipe out his assets. In this case, even though his assets exceed the limit, a decision that recovery of the overpayment would defeat the purpose of Title II would be justified.

Example 5: Charlie and Maureen were overpaid $1,600. They have $5,900 in a savings account. Their only income is Social Security of $600. Their monthly expenses are $600. A split decision can be made on this overpayment. Social Security can recover $900 to reduce their total assets to $5,000. The remaining $700 overpayment can be waived because reducing their assets below $5,000 will defeat the purpose of Title II.

Example 6: Bob and Dale were notified that they were overpaid $500. They claimed that they were without fault in causing the overpayment and that they were unable to repay. Social Security learned that they still had the $500 in Social Security benefits deposited in a savings account. Recovery of the overpayment would not defeat the purpose of Title II. However, if they had used $300 to pay debts, this portion of the overpayment might justify the finding of defeat the purpose of Title II. They would still be responsible to repay the remaining $200.

GUIDELINES ON ASSETS

Section 1108

If all your income is required for your support (see Sec. 1109), Social Security will look at your assets to decide if recovery of an overpayment would defeat the purpose of Title II. (see Sec. 1107.)

Generally, Social Security will not require you to reduce your assets below $3,000 to pay back an overpayment. If you have a dependent, the guideline is $5,000. You can allow an additional $600 for each additional dependent. For instance, the guideline for a person with two dependents is $5,600.

Example: You are overpaid $2,500. You are without fault and you need all your income for your support. You have no dependent, but your assets are $4,000. Social Security will waive recovery of $1,500, but require repayment of $1,000, the amount by which your assets exceed the guidelines.

Social Security has some flexibility with these guidelines, depending on the circumstances.

Example: Harry has assets over the guidelines. However, his wife is seriously ill. There are outstanding medical bills that, when paid, will reduce the assets below $5,000. More medical bills are anticipated, which will soon wipe out the remaining assets. Harry's present assets will not preclude a finding of defeat the purpose of Title II.

Assets include all liquid assets, such as bank accounts, stocks, bonds, etc., and the reasonable value of non-liquid assets, such as real estate. Social Security does not include household furnishings, clothes, the family car, or a home of reasonable value. Income-producing real estate is not included because the income from it is considered in evaluating your income and expenses. (see Sec. 1109.)

Social Security does include assets resulting from a pending inheritance, even if the money is not yet received. If you are a beneficiary of a trust fund, the amount in the fund is also included, even if the money is not immediately available.

GUIDELINES ON INCOME AND EXPENSES

Section 1109

To be eligible for waiver of an overpayment on the ground that recovery would defeat the purpose of Title II (see Sec. 1107), you first must show that you need all of your income to meet your living expenses. Social Security has flexibility when considering your income and expenses. They do not wish to significantly lower your standard of living if this would cause a hardship. However, they will not accept expenditures which are beyond the ordinary and necessary living expenses for food, clothing and shelter.

If you receive cash public assistance, recovery of the overpayment will be deemed to defeat the purpose of Title II. This includes SSI payments, VA disability pensions and Aid to Dependant Children (AFDC). If any person in the household receives AFDC, then recovery will defeat the purposes of Title II for all members of the household who were considered when the AFDC was granted.

Income from all sources is counted, including the income of a spouse and other dependent relatives living in the same house, whether or not they receive benefits.

The amount of reasonable expenses depends on the cost-of-living for your area. The knowledge and judgment of the local Social Security employee reviewing your case is considered. Expenses include those incurred for food, clothing, rent, mortgage payments, utilities, maintenance, life, accident and health insurance premiums, taxes, installment payments, medical and drug bills, child support, charitable contributions, newspapers, cigarettes, household supplies, gasoline, and other miscellaneous expenses.

Expenses to purchase or maintain non-essential items such as a boat or vacation home are not counted.

If a debt will be paid off in the near future, this will also be considered.

If your allegations about your living expenses, income, or assets appear incorrect, Social Security will require you to produce evidence to prove them.

If your expenses are higher than your income, Social Security will want to know how you meet them. If you cannot produce evidence of this, such as a dwindling bank account, they will not believe you.

If your monthly expenses are less than $100 plus $75 for each dependent, Social Security will presume they are reasonable and necessary.

These are not hard and fast rules about the types of acceptable evidence. If the evidence that you first submit appears convincing, you will not be required to produce any better evidence that may be available. Examples of evidence commonly accepted are letters from employers, copies of tax returns, tax receipts and bills, installment payment books, etc.

THE COMPROMISE SETTLEMENT

Section 1110

SSA has authority to accept compromise settlements in which the amount of the overpayment is not greater than $20,000. This means that they may accept less than the total overpayment in full settlement. In that case, there will be no further recovery of the balance. An offer to settle an overpayment greater than $20,000 will be referred to the Justice Department or the General Accounting Office.

Social Security cannot compromise an overpayment claim if the overpayment resulted from fraud, unless the overpaid person is deceased and the overpayment is $5,000 or less. However, if someone else who is still alive contributed to the fraud, the claim cannot be compromised regardless of the amount.

A claim to recover an overpayment may be compromised only if one of the following conditions exist:

1. you are unable to repay the full amount within a reasonable time, or the Government is unable to enforce collection within a reasonable time;

2. there is real doubt about the Government's ability to prove its case in court; or

3. the cost of collecting the claim is likely to exceed the amount of recovery (this is presumed if the difference between the compromise offer and the amount of the overpayment is less than $500.00).

A compromise offer must be in writing and must be signed by the overpaid person. An offer signed by an attorney may also be accepted if it appears that he is in a position to carry out its terms.

The written statement should include:

1. the reason a lesser amount has been offered;
2. the overpaid person's name, claim number (see Sec. 1407), and current address;
3. the total amount of overpayment;
4. the amount offered as a compromise;
5. when and how the compromise amount will be refunded (it should be within thirty days after acceptance of the offer); and
6. an understanding that if the compromise is not timely paid in a timely fashion, the full amount will be due.

Once the offer is made, it will take several months to get an answer. The decision whether to accept it is not made in the District Office. It is referred to a Program Service Center or to the Office of Disability Operations. (see Sec. 102.) If Social Security does not accept the offer, they may make a counteroffer.

Guidelines for Accepting Compromise Offers

Social Security will first decide if they have authority to compromise. (see Sec. 1110.) If so, they will consider whether they can recover the overpayment by withholding checks within the next three months. If so, the offer to settle should be at least eighty percent of the total overpayment.

If enforced collection is not possible, an offer of fifty percent of the overpayment will usually be accepted if you are financially unable to repay in full. An offer of less than fifty percent may be accepted if you are financially unable to pay more than the amount offered.

If you are financially able to repay in full, but enforced collection is not possible, an offer of sixty percent will usually be accepted.

These guidelines are simply that; they are not binding rules. Social Security has discretion to accept or reject any compromise offer. There are no appeal rights from a rejection of an offer to compromise.

If a request for waiver of overpayment (see Sec. 1104) or an appeal from the overpayment determination is pending, no action will be taken on the compromise offer until the outcome.

REPAYMENT

Section 1111

If you are not eligible for waiver of an overpayment (see Sec. 1104), and there is no compromise settlement (see Sec. 1110), the overpayment must be repaid. When Social Security notifies you that you are overpaid, they demand repayment in full.

If you are a beneficiary, they will tell you that your checks will be withheld until the overpayment is recovered in full.

Nevertheless, Social Security will accept installments (see Sec. 1114) or impose only partial monthly deductions (see Sec. 1113) if you ask them to do this.

No interest is charged on overpayments, no matter how long you take to repay.

DEDUCTIONS

Section 1112

Social Security may withhold your monthly benefits to recover an overpayment. They always propose to withhold benefits in full until the total amount is recovered. If you ask, however, they will usually agree to withhold only part of the monthly benefits. They will do this provided that the full overpayment will be recovered within twelve months, and the partial withholding is at least $10 per month.

If recovery by partial withholding for twelve months would cause a financial hardship, Social Security may extend the period, but no longer than thirty-six months. They will require financial information from you to explain the hardship. Interest is never charged on past due amounts.

INSTALLMENTS

Section 1113

Social Security will accept repayment of an overpayment in monthly installments, instead of deductions from your checks, if you ask for this arrangement. The same rules that apply to partial monthly deductions (see Sec. 1112) also apply to installments.

MEDICARE 12

MEDICARE IN GENERAL

Section 1201

Medicare is the health insurance program under the auspices of the Health Care Financing Administration, a branch of the Department of Health and Human Services. Medicare is no longer technically under the jurisdiction of the Social Security Administration (SSA), although SSA is a primary source of information, applications, and claims for Medicare. All questions on Medicare can be answered by contacting any Social Security office, or a toll-free number: 800-638-6833.

Medicare is divided into two parts: Hospital Insurance (sometimes referred to as *Part A*), and Medical Insurance (sometimes referred to as *Part B*).

Hospital Insurance is financed through a portion of the FICA payroll deduction from the paychecks of workers. Medical Insurance is partially financed through the collection of monthly premiums. These are either deducted from Social

Security checks or paid directly by covered individuals. (See Appendix 12 for the amount of the premiums.)

Hospital Insurance

Section 1202

Hospital insurance pays for four basic areas of medical care: in-patient care in a hospital; medically necessary in-patient care in a skilled nursing facility immediately following hospitalization (most nursing homes are not skilled nursing facilities); home health care; and hospice care.

All hospital insurance claims are paid on the basis of benefit periods. The first benefit period begins with the first hospitalization, but ends sixty calendar days after the termination of Medicare services (hospitalization, a skilled nursing facility, or rehabilitation services). There is no limit to the number of benefit periods an individual can have under hospital insurance.

Medicare hospital insurance does not pay for the entire stay in the hospital. In each benefit period, Medicare pays for all covered services for the first through the sixtieth day, except for the average cost of one day's hospitalization. For the sixty-first through ninetieth day in the hospital, Medicare pays for all covered services except for one-quarter of the average cost of each day in the hospital.

In addition, every Medicare beneficiary is entitled to sixty life-time reserve days. For life-time reserve days, Medicare pays for all covered services except for the cost of half of the average cost for each day in the hospital. (See Appendix 12 for these co-payment amounts.)

MEDICAL INSURANCE

Section 1203

Medicare medical insurance pays for six basic areas of medical care:

1. doctor's services, both in the doctor's office and in the hospital;

2. out-patient hospital care;

3. out-patient physical and speech therapy;

4. home health care;

5. ambulances.; and

6. medically necessary durable medical equipment, such as wheelchairs.

All payments under Medicare Part B are based on reasonable charges, not the current charges made by the physicians. Reasonable charges are determined by comparing the customary charge made by each doctor in the previous calendar year for each service with the "prevailing rate" for each service. The prevailing rate is the amount that will cover the customary charge in seventy-five percent of the bills submitted to Medicare in the previous year.

Medicare medical insurance pays eighty percent of the reasonable charge, after a predetermined deductible has been met, based on covered services, i.e., what Medicare would have paid. This may be different from the doctor's fee. All deductibles for Medicare Part B are based on the calendar year.

Premiums

You must pay a monthly premium for Medical Insurance. (See Appendix 12 for the amount.) If you do not elect to be covered by Medical Insurance when you first become eligible, you can enroll only during a General Enrollment Period. (see Sec. 407.)

If more than twelve months have passed since the close of your Initial Enrollment Period, you must pay an extra ten percent for each full twelve month period beginning with the first month after the Initial Enrollment Period and ending with the last month of the General Enrollment Period in which you apply.

Example: John became sixty-five and otherwise eligible for Medical Insurance in January 1992, but he did not enroll for Part B until January 15, 1992, during a General Enrollment Period. His Initial Enrollment Period closed in April 1992, the third month after his sixty-fifth birthday. (see Sec. 407.)

The months considered for the premium increase are May 1992 through March 1994. There are twenty-three months in this period, which is only one full twelve month period. His monthly premium will be increased by ten percent (rounded to the nearest ten cents).

For purposes of figuring the extra premium, you do not count any months during which you were covered both by Hospital Insurance (Part A) and an employer group health plan. (see Sec. 1204.)

PRIVATE HEALTH INSURANCE

Section 1204

Medicare is designed to provide basic protection against the very high cost of health care, but it will never pay all of your medical expenses. Because of this, many private insurance companies offer different protection in their policies. You should shop and compare different companies to determine which policy would be best for you.

For example, if you need several prescriptions, perhaps a company that covers prescription costs would be more advantageous. Other plans may offer eyeglass or dental plans. There is no one supplemental health plan that is best for everybody.

If you are older than sixty-five and you (or your spouse) work for an employer who has twenty or more employees, your employer is required to offer you the same health insurance benefits that he is offering to his young workers. If you continue to work after sixty-five, you have a choice of either accepting or rejecting your employer's health plan.

If you accept it, Medicare will become a secondary health insurance plan for you; your employer's health plan would be the primary insurance plan (the first payer). If you drop Part B because you are covered by the private plan, you may re-enroll when the private coverage ends. (see Sec. 407.)

You have the option of rejecting your employer's health plan, and if you do, Medicare will become your primary health insurance plan.

WHAT IS NOT COVERED

Section 1205

Medicare hospital insurance pays for all routine care in a hospital, including semi-private room, all your meals and regular nursing service, lab tests, and X-rays. It does not cover other items that are purely for personal convenience, such as the television, a radio, or a telephone. It will not pay the charge for private duty nurses or extra charges for a private room unless it is determined to be medically necessary, for example, to isolate a contagious disease.

Medicare medical insurance will not pay for the following services:

1. routine physical examinations and tests related to routine physical examination;

2. routine foot care;

3. eye or hearing examinations for prescribing or fitting eyeglasses or hearing aids. (Medicare will pay for some eye services related to cataract surgery);

4. immunizations;

5. most cosmetic surgery; and

6. most dental care, (dental care will be covered only if it involves surgery of the jaw or the setting of fractures of the jaw, or facial bones).

The above sections are by no means a comprehensive list of what is or is not covered by Medicare. For more complete information, you may obtain a copy of the Medicare Handbook published by Social Security.

ASSIGNMENT OF BENEFITS

Section 1206

Assignment of benefits is a procedure by which the doctor agrees to accept direct payment from Medicare for services he or she provides you. If a doctor accepts an assignment, he or she agrees to accept the amount that Medicare approves as his or her full charge for the service. Medicare will then pay eighty percent of that amount. You are still responsible to pay the twenty percent that Medicare does not pay.

WHEN TO FILE CLAIMS

Section 1207

Virtually all services rendered by hospitals and skilled nursing facilities are submitted directly to Medicare by the hospital. They will receive payment directly. You will receive only a notice of how much is paid and what the covered services are.

Some physicians, whether or not they accept assignment, will forward the claim for reimbursement to Medicare. If the physician does forward the claim to Medicare and has accepted assignment, you will receive an explanation of how much money was paid to the physician.

If the physician does not accept assignment, you will receive an explanation of how much Medicare pays along with a check.

You may forward your bills to Medicare as soon as you receive them, or you may save and submit them all at once. Since many people have a tendency to save their bills until the deductible is met or to save up their bills for the entire year and submit them all at once, the last three months of the year and the first three months of the year are very busy for Medicare. It may take a substantially longer time to process your request for reimbursement during these months.

It is generally advisable to submit your Medicare claims on a "flow" basis. As soon as you receive the service, submit the bill.

PROCESSING OF CLAIMS

Section 1208

Claims for Medicare medical insurance benefits are not processed by either SSA or the Health Care Financing Administration. These are processed by various private health insurance companies throughout the country. These companies are known as Medicare carriers.

For example, all Medicare Part B claims for services provided by doctors in Alabama will be forwarded to Medicare Blue Cross/Blue Shield of Alabama in Birmingham. Claims in the State of Hawaii are sent to Medicare Aetna Life and Casualty Company in Honolulu. You are told who your carrier is when you become entitled to Medicare.

If you do forward the Medicare claim to the wrong office, that office will forward it to the correct one.

THE MEDICARE CARD

Section 1209

Everyone entitled to Medicare hospital insurance or medical insurance is issued a red-white-and-blue card, entitled *Health Insurance Social Security Act*. This is known as the *Medicare card*. The information on the card includes your name, your Social Security claim number, and your sex. It indicates whether you are entitled to hospital insurance benefits only, medical insurance benefits only, or both. It also shows the effective date.

You are issued only one Medicare card, which is good for as long as you are entitled. Social Security will issue replacements only if your card is lost or stolen. It normally takes about four to six weeks after your initial application for Medicare is processed to receive the card. If you need to use Medicare before you receive it, the Social Security office can issue you a temporary letter of eligibility that will contain the information on the Medicare card. This can be used by the doctors and hospitals instead of a card.

APPEALS 13

APPEALS IN GENERAL

Section 1301

Social Security regulations establish an appeals process that must be followed if you wish to appeal a decision in your case. Not every administrative action may be appealed. (see Sec. 1302.) The appeals process has different levels: the reconsideration, the hearing, and the Appeals Council review. You must go through this process before a federal court will review your case.

You have the right to be represented by an attorney at any stage in your dealings with the Social Security Administration (SSA). This is not usually necessary unless you have a problem. You should be represented if you go to the hearing stage of the appeals process. An attorney may charge you a fee, if the amount has been approved by SSA. (see Sec. 1310.)

The legal rules of evidence do not apply in these administrative proceedings. This means that you may submit any evidence you wish, even if it is not admissible in a court of law.

WHAT YOU CAN AND CANNOT APPEAL

Section 1302

You can appeal only an *initial determination*. This is a formal decision affecting benefits, a period of disability, your earnings record, or entitlement to Medicare. Claims for payment under medical insurance (Medicare Part B) are not reviewed by SSA. Disputes about such payments are reviewed by the insurance company that administers medical insurance in your state. These cases cannot be reviewed in federal court.

Initial determinations include: awards or disallowances of monthly benefit claims; computations and recomputations of monthly benefit amounts; decisions on deductions from benefits and termination of benefits; *representative payee* (see Sec. 1414) determinations; overpayment decisions; and determinations about your earnings record.

Whenever an initial determination is made concerning your case, you will receive a written notice. This may be an award certificate, a disallowance letter, or a letter explaining the decision. The date of this letter starts the time limit for a request for reconsideration. (see Sec. 1308.)

Administrative decisions that are not initial determinations include: payment of combined checks (see Sec. 1004); withholding of part of a monthly benefit to recover an overpayment; and authorizing the amount of an attorney's fee. Any administrative action that is not an initial determination cannot be appealed through the normal appeals process, and is not reviewable in court.

THE RECONSIDERATION

Section 1303

The first step in the administrative appeals process is the reconsideration. You or your representative, such as an attorney, may request it. The request may also be filed by another person whose benefit rights are adversely affected by a determination made in your case.

You do not have to fill out the forms yourself. The Claims Representative (see Sec. 105) will do this for you, but you or your representative must sign them.

If you are appealing a disability denial, you should bring with you the names and addresses of all your treating doctors and hospitals. Be prepared to describe in detail any change in your condition, and how it affects your daily activities.

You may submit any evidence you wish. Copies of medical reports and hospital records will be accepted, unless they appear to be altered.

The reconsideration is a review of your record by a member of a different staff from the one that made the initial determination. You do not usually have the right to appear in person, although an experimental project is being conducted in certain parts of the country that allows you to be present and give testimony. In overpayment cases you may appear for a personal conference instead of the usual reconsideration. (see Sec. 1304.)

The request for a reconsideration must be filed within sixty days of the notice of the initial determination. (see Sec. 1308.)

THE PERSONAL CONFERENCE— OVERPAYMENT CASES

Section 1304

If your appeal is from a denial of your request for waiver of an overpayment (see Chapter 11), you may have a personal conference instead of a reconsideration. The personal conference is usually conducted by a Claims Representative (see Sec. 105) at your local District Office. You may appear (with an attorney if you wish) and explain your case. Any evidence that you wish to submit will be considered.

The personal conference must be requested within sixty days of the notice of the initial determination. (see Sec. 1308.)

THE HEARING

Section 1305

The hearing is the single most important step in the appeals process. It is conducted by an Administrative Law Judge (ALJ). The ALJ will independently review your case on the basis of the evidence in the file, any evidence you submit, and your sworn testimony.

You may appear in person and be represented by an attorney. The proceedings will be recorded on a tape recorder, not by a stenographer. A hearing assistant may be present to operate the recording system.

The administrative law judge may arrange for the testimony of expert witnesses called on behalf of the government. Vocational experts are frequently utilized in disability cases. You may produce your own experts to testify, but you are responsible for any fee. You may also request for the ALJ to issue subpoenas requiring the attendance and testimony of witnesses, or the production of documents or other evidence. Any such request for subpoenas should be made as far in advance of the hearing as possible (and no less than five days before the hearing).

Notice of the time and place of the hearing is sent to you at least ten days in advance. If you have a lawyer, call him or her as soon as you receive your notice to make sure that he received one as well.

In disability cases, it is very important for you to appear in person. The judge will ask you about your limitations, your medical treatments and medications, your work background, and your daily activities, among other things.

You must be fully prepared to answer these questions. We cannot discuss all of the questions you may be asked, but your lawyer will go over them with you before the hearing.

Be as specific and complete as possible in your answers, but never exaggerate. The judge will be looking for this. You should be able to describe how much weight, in pounds, you are able to lift and carry, how long you can sit, stand, and walk, and whether you have limitations bending, climbing, pushing, or pulling.

If you suffer from pain, be prepared to describe it as sharp or dull, to describe its frequency and location, what activities produce or aggravate it, and what relieves it. You should describe any side effects from medication, such as drowsiness, nausea, or impaired concentration.

The hearing will usually last about an hour. If you wish to submit additional evidence, you may request that the judge hold the record open for a week or two.

The judge will make a written decision on your case within a month after the hearing. If you win, you will receive benefits about a month later.

The request for hearing must be filed within sixty days of the reconsideration denial. (see Sec. 1308.) Your hearing will be scheduled within two or three months.

APPEALS COUNCIL REVIEW

Section 1306

You may request review of the administrative law judge's decision within sixty days. The Appeals Council may also review the decision of its own initiative within the same time.

The Appeals Council may deny your request for review, which it does in most cases. If so, the decision of the administrative law judge is the final decision of SSA.

If the Appeals Council believes that a significant question of law or policy is involved in your case, it may grant review. In some cases it may allow you or your lawyer to appear before it in Washington, D.C., to present oral arguments. Then, the Appeals Council will make its decision, which is final.

Sometimes cases are referred back to the administrative law judge to obtain additional evidence. This is called a remand. The ALJ will make another decision, which again may be reviewed by the Appeals Council.

COURT REVIEW

Section 1307

The Social Security Act provides that a federal district court has the authority to review any final decision of SSA if it was rendered after a hearing. This means that you must go through the administrative appeals process before going to court.

After the district court reviews your case, it can affirm, reverse, or send it back to Social Security for further proceedings (remand).

The court's review is limited to determining if the decision is supported by substantial evidence or if it contains an error of law. If there is any evidence to support the decision, you will lose, unless there is a legal error.

For example, if the administrative law judge chose to give more weight to one doctor's report (saying that you are not disabled) than to another doctor's report (saying that you are disabled), the court will uphold him. He is considered the *fact-finder*, and his conclusions will not be disturbed if supported by more than a "scintilla of evidence;" i.e., such evidence as a reasonable mind might accept as adequate to support a conclusion.

If there is error in his application of the law to the facts of your case, the court may overturn his decision. Such cases may result in a remand to the administrative law judge to determine additional facts in light of the correct rule of law.

A legal action seeking review of a final decision must be filed in federal district court within sixty days. The court's filing fee is currently $60. Any legal fees must be approved by the court.

TIME LIMITS

Section 1308

A request for a reconsideration, hearing, or Appeals Council review must be filed within sixty days of the prior decision. The time limit for filing a civil action in federal court is the same.

The time starts running from the date you receive the notice of the decision. This is presumed to be five days after the notice is mailed.

A protective filing statement (see Sec. 402) will stop the running of the time limit for administrative appeals, but not for the civil action. It must clearly indicate an intent to appeal. No formal words are required; simply write "I wish to appeal the decision in my case."

The time limit for requesting an administrative review may be extended if you have *good cause* for late filing, for example, if you were hospitalized, or if you never received the notice of the decision.

The time limit for filing a civil action may be extended by the Appeals Council. A request for extension should be filed before the time limit expires. If not, the request may be granted if you have good cause for being late.

If a time limit expires on a Saturday, Sunday, legal holiday, or Federal nonwork day, the time limit is extended to the following work day.

REOPENING CLOSED CASES

Section 1309

A decision that has become final may be reopened and revised for any reason within twelve months of the notice of the initial determination.

A decision may be reopened within four years for the following reasons:

- if new evidence is found after the initial determination;

- if a clerical error was made in figuring a benefit amount;

- if the initial determination was clearly wrong based on the evidence in file;or

- if there is good cause.

Good cause does not exist in situations in which the only basis for reopening is a change of legal interpretation.

A determination may be reopened at any time for the following reasons:

- if fraud or similar fault was involved;

- if someone else makes a conflicting claim on the same earnings record;

- for survivor benefits if the worker was presumed dead and is found alive, or is now presumed dead because of unexplained absence for seven years;

- if a worker's earnings record now shows that a previous denial for insufficient earnings was wrong;

- if an unfavorable decision was based on a clerical error apparent on the face of the evidence in file; or

- if errors were made involving railroad employment or military wage credits causing duplicate payments or the failure to give proper credit.

ATTORNEYS

Section 1310

Usually, you do not require an attorney to handle your Social Security affairs, although you have the right to be represented at any time. You may require an attorney if your claim has been denied or if you have incurred a substantial overpayment.

Business owners who plan to claim retirement benefits should consult attorneys before giving any statements to Social Security. (see Sec. 811.)

If you wish to consult or retain a lawyer, it is important to find one who is well-versed in the area of Social Security. Few lawyers practice in this field, although the number is growing.

The Bar Association in your county may be able to refer you to a suitable lawyer. Many lawyers who practice Worker's Compensation law also handle Social Security, especially disability cases.

You are responsible for the payment of your attorney's fee. Any fee for services rendered representing you must be approved by SSA.

If you win your case, SSA will withhold 25 percent of any past due benefits until an approved fee has been established. Most lawyers will accept a disability case on a contingent basis. This means that no fee will be charged if the case is unsuccessful.

When a fee has been approved, SSA will pay the attorney directly out of the withheld benefits. If there is any unused balance, it will be sent to you. If the approved fee is greater than the amount withheld, the lawyer will bill you.

Sometimes an attorney may require you to pay him a retainer in advance. If so, he must hold this in escrow (set apart from his own funds) until a fee has been approved. If the approved fee is less, he must return the difference to you.

MISCELLANEOUS PROVISIONS 14

SUPPLEMENTAL SECURITY INCOME (SSI)

Section 1401

The Supplemental Security Income (SSI) program was established in 1974. SSI benefits are payable to people age sixty-five and older, the blind, and the disabled who are in need. Social Security is an insurance program. SSI is a welfare program.

Entitlement to SSI is contingent upon the amount and types of income and resources you have available to you. The income and resources of those relatives legally responsible for your support (parents of minor children, spouses, etc.) will also affect your entitlement to SSI.

The dollar amount of SSI payments is fixed for all recipients (although many states include supplemental payments in the SSI check) but is affected by various factors, such as types and amounts of other income you receive, the value of your resources, and whether you live alone, with others, or in a nursing or group home.

The SSI check is gold-colored and is delivered on the first day of the month. Although the SSI program is administered by the Social Security Administration (SSA), the SSI payments do not come from the Social Security trust fund. The payments are made from the general revenues of the Federal Government derived from various tax payments. If you think you are eligible for SSI or require more information, you should contact your local Social Security office.

BLACK LUNG BENEFITS

Section 1402

The Federal Coal Mine Health and Safety Act of 1969 established payments to coal miners who suffer from pneumoconiosis, commonly referred to as *Black Lung*. Only Black Lung claims filed before July 1, 1973, are under the jurisdiction of Social Security.

All applications filed after that date are under the jurisdiction of the Department of Labor. Social Security does maintain jurisdiction of claims filed by the survivors of miners who were afflicted with Black Lung.

SSA makes Black Lung payments to coal miners who are totally disabled due to pneumoconiosis. Additional payments may be made to these miners to provide for dependent wives, divorced wives, or children. Survivor benefits may be paid to widows, children, surviving divorced wives, parents, brothers or sisters of a miner. These benefits may be paid if a miner was entitled to Black Lung benefits at the time of his death, if he was totally disabled by pneumoconiosis at the time of death, or if he died from pneumoconiosis. For further information, contact Social Security or the Department of Labor.

Benefit Estimates

Section 1403

SSA provides estimates of the amount of benefits payable to anyone who requests such information. All benefit estimates given by Social Security are based on the amount of earnings, actually shown on the record of earnings and not on any proposed future earnings.

Although Social Security provides estimates for people of any age, estimates for workers who are under sixty cannot be completely accurate. Estimates for people of any age can only be based on the information currently available to Social Security. Estimates of benefits far into the future have been shown to be inaccurate because of changes in the Social Security Act and wide swings in inflation.

If you are nearing retirement age and would like an estimate, you may contact your Social Security office.

Obtaining Your Earnings Record

Section 1404

Social Security will provide, free of charge, a *Statement of Earnings*. This statement shows the annual earnings credited to your record. Because of the amount of time it takes to process reports of earnings, the first and second year preceding the request may not be available. It is a good idea to check your Social Security records every three years.

CORRECTING YOUR EARNINGS RECORD

Section 1405

Usually, the earnings record can only be corrected for up to three years, three-month, and fifteen days after the year the wages were paid or self-employment income was earned. If you have a disagreement with your employer about how much you were paid, when you were paid, or whether the work was covered under Social Security, you must act within the three year, three-month,s and fifteen-day time limit.

If a disagreement exists, Social Security will help you obtain the necessary information to settle the dispute. Based on all evidence received, Social Security will decide whether earnings can be credited, how much earnings should be credited, and for what period. Social Security will notify you of the decision they have reached, and of what corrective action, if any, they are taking.

Once the three-year, three-month, fifteen day time limit has expired, the earnings record cannot be revised unless one of the following conditions is met:

1. an entry was established through fraud;

2. a mechanical, clerical, or other obvious error is detected (such as earnings mistakenly reported under an incorrect Social Security number or mistakenly unreported);

3. earnings were credited to the wrong person or to the wrong period;

4. to transfer earnings to or from the Railroad Retirement Board if reported to the wrong agency;

5. to add wages paid by an employer who made no report of any wages paid to an employee;

6. to add or remove wages in accordance with a wage report filed by an employer;

7. to add self-employment income if the tax return was filed within the legal time limit; and

8. to add self-employment income up to the amount of employee wages deleted as being erroneously reported if a self-employment tax return is filed within three years, three months, and fifteen days of the year the earnings were deleted. (This may occur if *employment* later is determined to be *self-employment*.)

Social Security does its best to ensure that wages are properly reported. Although corrections legally can be made at a later time, the longer you wait to correct a problem, the harder it will be, due to destruction and loss of records. You should take action to correct your Social Security record as soon as a problem is identified.

REPORTING CHANGE OF ADDRESS

Section 1406

A change of address can be reported to Social Security using three methods—a telephone call, an office visit, or a letter.

The Department of the Treasury prepares and mails all Government checks. Social Security must notify the Treasury Department of all address changes. Social Security checks are delivered to the local post offices well in advance of the due date to ensure their timely delivery.

All of these factors take time. It can require as much as forty to forty-five days for a change of address to take effect. It is important to notify Social Security as soon as you know your new address. It is also important to file a change of address form with the Post Office so that even if the change of address does not register, the Post Office can forward your check.

CLAIM NUMBERS AND BENEFICIARY IDENTIFICATION CODES

Section 1407

Every person who applies for Social Security benefits is assigned a claim number, and all records are maintained by that number. The claim number consists of the Social Security number of the worker on whose account the benefits are based, with a letter (or letter and number) following it. It is used on all correspondence from Social Security.

The retirement beneficiary's claim number is his Social Security number followed by the letter A. His wife on his account is assigned his number followed by the letter B (if she is sixty-two or older) or B2 (if she receives because she has a child in her care). Children are identified by the letter C and a number (usually one for the youngest, two for the next youngest, etc.). Widows receiving on account of age are identified by the letter D.

If a person is entitled on more than one account, the records are maintained under both accounts, but one account takes precedence. If a woman receives both as a retired wage earner and as a widow, all correspondence and checks will be sent to her in her own number followed by the letter A. Other than the initial award letter, the secondary account number will not be mentioned. Beneficiary identification code letters are listed in Appendix 8.

WHO IS ENTITLED TO BENEFITS DUE TO A DECEASED BENEFICIARY

Section 1408

An underpayment exists when benefits are due to a person but have not been paid. Usually, underpayments are due because of returned checks or increases in benefit amounts for various reasons. If the underpaid person is alive, the payment is made to him (or to his representative).

A deceased person can also be due an underpayment. When this occurs, the underpayment is paid to whichever person is highest in priority in the following list:

1. to the widow or widower, if either were living in the same household at the time of death, or entitled to monthly benefits on the same earnings record (receiving spouse's benefits);

2. to the child(ren) of the underpaid person entitled to monthly benefits on the same earnings record as the

deceased for the month of death. The underpayment is divided equally among all such children;

3. to the parent(s) of the underpaid person entitled to monthly benefits on the same earnings record for the month of death;

4. to the widow who was neither living with the underpaid person nor entitled to monthly benefits on the same earnings record;

5. to the child(ren) who were not entitled to monthly benefits on the same earnings record as the deceased for the month of death;

6. to the parent(s) who were not entitled to monthly benefits on the same account as the deceased; or

7. to the legal representative of the estate.

For example, if the deceased was survived by his wife, who was living with him but not entitled to monthly Social Security benefits, and an eighteen year old daughter who was receiving monthly Social Security benefits on his account, the underpayment would be paid to his widow. If the deceased and his wife were separated, the underpayment would be paid to his daughter. If the daughter was not entitled to monthly benefits and no one else was, the underpayment would be payable to the widow.

The underpayment is not paid to all persons on the list of priority. It is paid only to the highest person on the list. Two or more people with the same priority (e.g., two surviving children) split the underpayment equally.

If Social Security can determine who is entitled to the underpayment, they will pay it automatically, without a specific request. If the Social Security records are insufficient to determine all persons who may be entitled (surviving wife or children not entitled to monthly benefits) a request is required from one person who is entitled to share in the underpayment. If the underpayment is over $400, proof of relationship may be required.

TAXATION OF SOCIAL SECURITY BENEFITS

Section 1409

Social Security benefits are subject to income tax if you have income which exceeds the following amounts: $25,000, if you file as a single taxpayer; $32,000, if you are married and file a joint return; but $0, if you are married and you live with your spouse at any time during the year and file separate returns.

When you figure your total Social Security benefits received, you have to include gross benefits before deductions for such items as the Medicare premium, a lawyer's fee, or Worker's Compensation offsets.

In figuring your total income, you must also include "non-taxable" earnings such as interest from municipal bonds. The Social Security benefits are taxable only to the extent they exceed the above limits, but for an individual only 50 percent of the excess is taxable up to $34,000, 85 percent of the excess over $34,000; for a couple, 50 percent of the excess over $32,000 and up to $44,000, then 85 percent of the excess over $44,000.

If you wish, you may request that taxes be withheld from your benefits. To have your taxes withheld, you must: Complete IRS Form W-4V, called a Voluntary Withholding Request form. You may select what percentage of your monthly benefit amount you want withheld either 7 percent, 15 percent, 28 percent or 31 percent. Only these percentages can be used. Flat dollar amounts are not acceptable. After you have made your selection, sign and return the form to your local Social Security office by mail or in person

IMMUNITY OF BENEFITS FROM CREDITORS

Section 1410

No creditor has the right to attach a Social Security benefit. The Social Security benefit can only be attached by the IRS for the payment of back taxes or for child support payments. Once the benefit has been received and put into an account, such as a savings account or a checking account, it may be attached unless it is a separate account clearly marked "Social Security Benefits."

It is very important, if you are receiving benefits on behalf of a child and placing them in a savings account that the account clearly specifies that the funds are Social Security funds. Then, your creditors cannot attach the child's money.

CRIMINAL PENALTIES FOR FRAUD

Section 1411

Under the Social Security program, fraud can be found to exist if a person furnishes false information as to identity to get a Social Security number, or a false statement in connection with a claim for Social Security benefits, or if a person uses a Social Security number obtained by fraud.

Fraud can also be found if a person conceals or fails to report any event affecting his or her right to receive a Social Security check, or if a person uses Social Security benefits received on behalf of one person for the use of somebody other than that person. Social Security may prosecute fraud even if no benefits were ever paid by the government on the basis of the statement.

The penalty for fraud ranges from a minimum of not more than a $500 fine or imprisonment of one year, or both, to a fine of not more than $10,000 or imprisonment for up to fifteen years, or both. Acts such as alleging that you have retired when you actually have not, or alleging that you have transferred a business to your spouse when you have not, are a couple of examples of cases that Social Security may prosecute.

FOREIGN SOCIAL SECURITY CREDIT

Section 1412

Social Security has entered into agreements with eighteen foreign countries: Austria, Belgium, Canada, Chile, Finland, France, Germany, Greece, Ireland, Italy, Luxembourg, Netherlands, Norway, Portugal, South Korea, Spain, Sweden,

Switzerland, and the United Kingdom. The agreements allow people who have work credit in those countries to file applications with Social Security in the United States for potential Social Security benefits from the other country.

This provision allows some people who do not have enough work under either Social Security system to be able to collect one Social Security benefit. It also allows people who are entitled to benefits from both systems to file for them and collect them conveniently.

At the time you file for Social Security benefits in the U.S., the interviewer will ask if you have ever worked in a foreign country covered by the agreement. Social Security will complete a second application for you for potential benefits from that other country for you.

RAILROAD EMPLOYMENT

Section 1413

People who work for the railroads are not covered under Social Security; they are covered by the Railroad Retirement Board (RRB). If you are entitled to benefits from both Social Security and from the RRB, they are made in one combined payment. SSA will compute your Social Security benefit and send the information to the RRB, who will figure your annuity and adjust it for the amount of Social Security you receive.

To be entitled to Railroad Retirement benefits, an employee must have ten years of railroad service. If he or she has less, his or her railroad employment will be credited to his or her Social

Security account. If an employee does not have enough work to collect a Social Security payment, his or her earnings under Social Security will be credited to his or her railroad retirement account. Survivor benefits may be paid by either agency.

More information on railroad retirement benefits can be obtained by writing to Information Service, U.S. Railroad Retirement Board, 844 Rush Street, Chicago, Illinois 60611, or by contacting RRB officials in major cities throughout the country.

RECEIVING BENEFITS FOR SOMEONE ELSE

Section 1414

Social Security benefits will be paid to an adult, in his or her own name, unless this adult has been shown to be incompetent or incapable of managing personal funds. A mentally ill person may still be able to manage benefits in his or her own interest; if so the payment will be made directly to him or her. A physically disabled person will have payments made to a representative payee only if so disabled as to be unable to manage benefit payments even with the help of someone else.

Benefits to children under the age of eighteen normally are made to a representative payee. The payment may be made directly to a child under the age of eighteen if the child is entirely self-supporting and living away from home, or in other limited circumstances. It is unusual for a child under the age of eighteen to collect payments on his or her own behalf. Once a child turns eighteen, payments are made directly to him or her, unless there is a need for a representative payee.

The order of preference in appointing a representative payee for a child is:

1) the natural or adoptive parent with custody or a court-appointed guardian;

2) the natural or adoptive parent who does not have custody of the child but who contributes to the child's support and demonstrates strong concern for the child's well-being;

3) a natural or adoptive parent who demonstrates a strong concern for the child's well-being;

4) a relative, including a stepparent, having custody of the child;

5) a relative who does not have custody of the child but who contributes to the child's support and demonstrates a strong concern for the child's well-being;

6) an authorized social agency; and

7) a relative or close friend who demonstrates strong concern for the child's well-being.

The order of preference for an adult is:

1) the legal guardian, spouse or other relative who has actual custody of the beneficiary or who demonstrates a strong concern for his welfare;

2) a friend who has custody, who demonstrates a strong concern for his welfare;

3) a public or non-profit agency or institution having custody of the beneficiary; and

4) a private institution operating for profit licensed under applicable state law having custody of the beneficiary, such as a nursing home.

The responsibilities of a representative payee are:

- to apply benefit payments for the beneficiary's use;

- to maintain a concern for the personal welfare of the beneficiary;

- to notify Social Security when the responsibility for the welfare and care of any person entitled to Social Security ends;

- to report to Social Security any changes that may affect the beneficiary's right to receive Social Security; and

- to give Social Security periodic written reports accounting for the use of benefits, if requested to do so. Benefits paid to a representative payee must be spent for the beneficiary's current needs or saved for the beneficiary if all current needs are being met.

If you receive Social Security benefits on behalf of another and find that you are able to save some to establish a bank account for the person, the bank account must clearly indicate that the funds in that account are Social Security benefits. The preferred format for the title of the account is: "Name of Beneficiary, By Name of Representative Payee," or "Name of Beneficiary, By Name of Representative Payee, Trustee."

NOTE: *A bank account title such as "Name of Payee in Trust for Beneficiary" should not be used because some states treat the funds in such an account as belonging to the Representative Payee.*

Whatever the title of the account is, it must clearly indicate that the money in the account is the property of the beneficiary, and no one else, and that it is Social Security benefits.

Social Security requires a written account from representative payees on a periodic basis. If you are acting as a representative payee, you should keep records showing how the Social Security money was spent. The reporting they will ask you for may include the amount of benefits you had at the beginning of the period, where the beneficiary lived during the period, the amount of income from other sources during the year, how the benefits were spent, how much of the Social Security benefits were saved and how they were invested.

APPENDICES

APPENDIX 1

List of Secondary Proof of Age

(see Sec. 410)

If no birth certificate or baptismal certificate recorded before age five is available, Social Security requires you to submit other documents to prove your age. This appendix is divided into two sections—First Priority Convincing Records, and Second Priority Convincing Records.

I - First Priority Convincing Records

If you submit one document from the list and the date of birth on that document agrees with the date of birth you gave Social Security when you applied for your Social Security Number, no other proof of age is necessary.

I-1. Family Bible or other family record recorded before age thirty-six.

I-2. School or School Census records recorded before age twenty-one.

I-3. 1910, 1920, or 1930 Federal Census record.

I-4. Domestic or Canadian delayed birth record established before age fifty-five.

I-5. State census records for 1905 or 1915.

I-6. Insurance Policies taken out before age twenty-one.

I-7. Immigration and Naturalization Service (INS) arrival records recorded before age thirty-one.

I-8. Religious records recorded before age eighteen.

I-9. Newspaper birth announcements.

II - Second Priority Convincing Records

If no First Priority Convincing Record (above) is available (as well as no birth or baptismal record recorded before age five) and you submit one document from this list, if the date of birth on that document agrees with the date of birth you gave Social Security when you applied for your Social Security Number, no other proof of age is necessary.

II-1. School records recorded after age twenty and before age fifty-five.

II-2. Baptismal record recorded after age seventeen and before age fifty-five.

II-3. 1925 State census records.

II-4. Domestic or Canadian delayed birth record established after age fifty-four - if the delayed birth record shows the basis for the date of birth.

II-5. Birth records for your children recorded before you were age thirty-one.

II-6. Marriage records recorded before age thirty-six.

II-7. Citizenship data recorded before age twenty-six.

II-8. World War II draft and discharge records recorded before age thirty-one.

II-9. Employment records established before age twenty-one.

II-10. Voting records established before age fifty-six.

II-11. Other records recorded before age twenty-one.

APPENDIX 2

Quarters of Coverage Required for Insured Status

Following is a chart showing the earnings required for a Quarter of Coverage and four charts which show the minimum number of Quarters of Coverage needed for Insured Status, according to the type of benefit.

Chart 1: Earnings Required for a Quarter of Coverage

Year	Amount
Pre-1978	$ 50
1978	250
1979	260
1980	290
1981	310
1982	340
1983	370
1984	390
1985	410
1986	440
1987	460
1988	470
1989	500
1990	520
1991	540
1992	570
1993	590
1994	620
1995	630
1996	640
1997	670
1998	700
1999	740
2000	780
2001	830
2002	870

Chart 2: Retirement Benefits

Year of Birth	Minimum Number of Quarters
1915	26
1916	27
1917	28
1918	29
1919	30
1920	31
1921	32
1922	33
1923	34
1924	35
1925	36
1926	37
1927	38
1928	39
1929 and later	40

Chart 3: Disability or Survivor Benefits for People Born Before 1930

Year of Onset of Disability or Death	Minimum Number of Quarters of Coverage Required
1970	19
1971	20
1972	21
1973	22
1974	23
1975	24
1976	25
1977	26
1978	27
1979	28
1980	29
1981	30
1982	31
1983	32
1984	33
1985	34
1986	35
1987	36
1988	37
1989	38
1990	39
1991 and later	40

Chart 4: Disability or Survivor Benefits for People Born in 1930 or Later

Age of Onset of Disability or Death	Minimum Number of Quarters of Coverage Required
28 and younger	6
29	7
30	8
31	9
32	10
33	11
34	12
35	13
36	14
37	15
38	16
39	17
40	18
41	19
42	20
43	21
44	22
45	23
46	24
47	25
48	26
49	27
50	28
51	29

(continued next page)

52	30
53	31
54	32
55	33
56	34
57	35
58	36
59	37
60	38
61	39
62 and older	40

Chart 5: Disability Insured Status (see Sec. 604)

Note: This chart shows the minimum number of quarters of coverage required in the calendar quarters immediately preceding onset of disability. For example, $^{15}/_{30}$ means that fifteen quarters of coverage are needed in the thirty calendar quarters ($7^1/_2$ years) before onset of disability. $^{20}/_{40}$ means that twenty quarters of coverage are needed in the forty calendar quarters (ten years before onset of disability).

Age at Onset of Disability	Minimum Number of Quarters of Coverage Required/Calendar Quarters Before Disability
24 and younger	6/12
24½	7/14
25	8/16
25½	9/18
26	10/20
26½	11/22
27	12/24
27½	13/26
28	14/28
28½	15/30
29	16/32
29½	17/34
30	18/36
30½	19/38
31	20/40

APPENDIX 3

FICA Yearly Maximums

(Maximum Earnings Subject to Social Security Tax)

Year	Earnings
1937 through 1950	$ 3,000
1951 through 1954	3,600
1955 through 1958	4,200
1959 through 1965	4,800
1966 through 1967	6,600
1968 through 1971	7,800
1972	9,000
1973	10,800
1974	13,200
1975	14,100
1976	15,300
1977	16,500
1978	17,700
1979	22,900
1980	25,900
1981	29,700
1982	32,400
1983	35,700
1984	37,800
1985	39,600
1986	42,000
1987	43,800
1988	45,000
1989	48,000

Year	Earnings
1990	51,300
1991	53,400
1992	55,500
1993	57,600
1994	60,600
1995	61,200
1996	62,700
1997	65,400
1998	68,400
1999	72,600
2000	76,200
2001	80,400
2002	84,900

Future maximums will be increased based on the rate of inflation and announced by the Social Security Administration in the fall of the preceding year.

NOTE: *The total FICA tax is 15.3 percent (half paid by the employer and half paid by the employee) of which 12.4 percent is for Old Age, Survivor and Disability Insurance. It is only this portion of the tax which is subject to the above limits. There is no maximum for earnings subject to the Hospital Insurance (Medicare) portion of the FICA tax, which is 2.9 percent, payable one half by the employer and half by the employee.*

APPENDIX 4

Monthly Benefits

Worker with steady earnings at the maximum level since age 22

Retirement at beginning of year	Retirement at age 62 Monthly benefit	Retirement at age 65 Monthly benefit	Age 70 Monthly benefit
1994	954	1,147	1,358
1995	972	1,199	1,474
1996	1,006	1,248	1,501
1997	1,056	1,326	1,609
1998	1,117	1,342	1,648
1999	1,191	1,373	1,684
2000	1,248	1,433	1,751
2001	1,314	1,538	1,877
2002	1,382	1,660	1,988

Worker with High Earnings

High earnings are defined as earnings equal to 160 percent of the national average wage index. Worker with steady, high earnings since age 22.

Retirement at beginning of year	Retirement at age 62 Monthly benefit	Retirement at age 65 Monthly benefit	Age 70 Monthly benefit
1994	881	1,057	1,225
1995	892	1,098	1,324
1996	918	1,137	1,344
1997	958	1,202	1,439
1998	1,008	1,210	1,471
1999	1,070	1,231	1,501
2000	1,115	1,278	1,553
2001	1,169	1,365	1,658
2002	1,224	1,467	1,748

Worker with Average Earnings

Average earnings are defined as earnings equal to the national average wage index. Worker with steady, average earnings since age 22.

Retirement at beginning of year	Retirement at age 62 Monthly benefit	Retirement at age 65 Monthly benefit	Age 70 Monthly benefit
1994	689	829	967
1995	696	858	1,043
1996	714	886	1,058
1997	743	933	1,129
1998	780	938	1,152
1999	825	953	1,174
2000	858	987	1,212
2001	897	1,051	1,291
2002	936	1,127	1,358

Worker with Low Earnings

Low earnings are defined as earnings equal to 45 percent of the national average wage index. Worker with steady, low earnings since age 22.

Retirement at beginning of year	Retirement at age 62 Monthly benefit	Retirement at age 65 Monthly benefit	Age 70 Monthly benefits
1994	418	505	579
1995	422	520	625
1996	433	537	634
1997	451	566	670
1998	473	568	692
1999	501	577	706
2000	520	597	729
2001	544	637	776
2002	568	682	815

APPENDIX 5

Reduction Factors (Sec. 703)

INTRODUCTORY NOTE: *The full Retirement Age, i.e. the age at which one may receive an unreduced retirement, spouse or widow's benefit has been increased effective with those born in 1938 and later (1940 for widows), on a gradually increasing basis. See Section 703 "Reductions" for a full discussion. Therefore, additional reduction months are applied to those turning sixty-two (sixty for widows) in 2000. For retirement and spouse benefits, the reduction factor for reduction months in excess of thirty-six is $5/12$ of one percent for each extra month. For widows, the factor remains the same.*

Chart 1: Retirement Benefits

Reduction Months	Reduction Factor	Reduction Months	Reduction Factor
1	.994	19	.894
2	.988	20	.888
3	.983	21	.883
4	.977	22	.877
5	.972	23	.872
6	.966	24	.866
7	.961	25	.861
8	.955	26	.855
9	.950	27	.850
10	.944	28	.844
11	.938	29	.838
12	.933	30	.833

Reduction Months	Reduction Factor	Reduction Months	Reduction Factor
13	.927	31	.827
14	.922	32	.822
15	.916	33	.816
16	.911	34	.811
17	.905	35	.805
18	.900	36	.800

Chart 2: Wife's Benefits

Reduction Months	Reduction Factor	Reduction Months	Reduction Factor
1	.993	19	.868
2	.986	20	.861
3	.979	21	.854
4	.972	22	.847
5	.965	23	.840
6	.958	24	.833
7	.951	25	.826
8	.944	26	.819
9	.937	27	.812
10	.930	28	.805
11	.923	29	.798
12	.916	30	.791
13	.909	31	.784
14	.902	32	.777

Reduction Months	Reduction Factor	Reduction Months	Reduction Factor
15	.895	33	.770
16	.888	34	.763
17	.881	35	.756
18	.875	36	.750

Chart 3: Widow's Benefits

Reduction Months	Reduction Factor	Reduction Months	Reduction Factor
1	.995	31	.853
2	.991	32	.848
3	.986	33	.843
4	.981	34	.839
5	.976	35	.834
6	.972	36	.829
7	.967	37	.824
8	.962	38	.820
9	.957	39	.815
10	.953	40	.810
11	.948	41	.805
12	.943	42	.801
13	.938	43	.796
14	.934	44	.791
15	.929	45	.786
16	.924	46	.782

Reduction Months	Reduction Factor	Reduction Months	Reduction Factor
17	.919	47	.777
18	.915	48	.772
19	.910	49	.767
20	.905	50	.763
21	.900	51	.758
22	.896	52	.753
23	.891	53	.748
24	.886	54	.744
25	.881	55	.739
26	.877	56	.734
27	.872	57	.729
28	.867	58	.725
29	.862	59	.720
30	.858	60	.715

APPENDIX 6: COST OF LIVING INCREASES

NOTE: *COLA increases are applicable for benefits paid in the year indicated in the chart. The effective month of COLA increases is December of the year preceeding.*

Year	Percentage
1992	3.7%
1993	3.0%
1994	2.6%
1995	2.8%
1996	2.6%
1997	2.9%
1998	2.1%
1999	1.31%
2000	2.4%
2001	3.5%
2002	2.6%

APPENDIX 7: EARNINGS LIMITS BY YEAR

Year	Age	Monthly	Yearly
1992	Under 65	$620	$ 7,440
	65 and Older	850	10,200
1993	Under 65	640	7,680
	65 and Older	880	10,560
1994	Under 65	670	8,040
	65 and Older	930	11,160
1995	Under 65	680	8,160
	65 and Older	940	11,280
1996	Under 65	690	8,280
	65 and Older	1041	12,500
1997	Under 65	720	8640
	65 and Older	1125	13,500
1998	Under 65	760	9,120
	65 and Older	1208	14,500*
1999	Under 65	800	9,600
	65 and Older	1291	15,500*
2000	Under 65	840	10,080
	65 and Older	1416	17,000*
2001	Under 65	890	10,680
	65 and Older	2083	25,000*
2002	Under 65	940	11,280
	65 and Older	2500	30,000*

* Public Law 104-121, enacted on March 29, 1996, increased the exempt amounts for beneficiaries aged 65-69, relative to amounts under prior law, by providing a schedule of fixed amounts through the year 2002. Exempt amounts for those under 65 will be established separately each year on a current basis. Note also that beginning with 2000, earnings after attainment of Full Retirement Age no longer affects benefits.

APPENDIX 8:

List of Most Common Beneficiary Identification Codes

A: Retirement on own work record

B: Aged Wife

B1:   Aged Husband

B2:   Young Wife (with child in care)

B6:   Divorced Wife

C: Child

D: Aged Widow

D1:   Aged Widower

D6:   Surviving Divorced Wife

E: Young Widow (mother)

E1:   Surviving Divorced Mother

E4:   Young Widower (father)

F: Parent

G: Lump Sum Claimant

HA: Disabled Worker

HB: Aged Wife of Disabled Worker

HB2: Young Wife of Disabled Worker

HC: Child of Disabled Worker

J: Prouty (special age 72 benefits)

K: Prouty (wife)

M: Medicare—Medical Insurance Only

T: Medicare Only—Both Parts

W: Disabled Widow

W1:   Disabled Widower

W6:   Surviving Disabled Divorced Wife

APPENDIX 9

Program Service Centers

These centers store folders and work on certain cases after they have been processed by a District Office. See discussion in Section102. Cases are assigned based on the first three digits of the social security claim number. Disability cases where the worker is under $59^1/_2$ go to the Office of Disability Operations (PSC-7). Cases where the claimant lives abroad are handled by the Division of International Operations (PSC-8).

Program Service Center No. & Initials	Social Security Account Number Breakdown (1st 3 digits)	Mailing Address
PSC-1 (NEPSC)	001-134	Social Security Administration Northeastern Program Service Center 96-05 Horace Harding Expressway Flushing, NY 11368
PSC-2 (MATPSC)	135-222 232-236 577-584	Social Security Administration Mid-Atlantic Program Service Center 300 Spring Garden St. Philadelphia, PA 19123
PSC-3 (SEPC)	223-231 237-267 400-428 587	Social Security Administration Southeastern Program Service Center 2001 12th Ave. N. Birmingham, AL 35285

Program Service Center No. & Initials	Social Security Account Number Breakdown (1st 3 digits)	Mailing Address
PSC-4 (GLPSC)	268-302 316-399 700 series	Social Security Administration Great Lakes Program Service Center 600 W. Madison St. Chicago, IL 60606
PSC-5 (WNPSC)	501-504 516-524 526-576 586	Social Security Administration Western Program Service Center BX 2000 Richmond, CA 94802
PSC-6 (MAMPSC)	303-315 429-500 505-515 525 585	Social Security Administration Mid-America Program Service Center 601 E. 12th Street Kansas City, MO 64106
PSC-7 (ODO)	All disability and end stage renal disease cases (under age 59$^{-1}/_2$)	Social Security Administration Office of Disability Operations Baltimore, MD 21241
PSC-8 (DIO)	Foreign Claims	Social Security Administration Division of International Operations BX 1756 Baltimore, MD 21203

APPENDIX 10: FORM SSA-735

DEPARTMENT OF HEALTH AND HUMAN SERVICES
SOCIAL SECURITY ADMINISTRATION

TOE 540

NOTICE OF MISSING SOCIAL SECURITY PAYMENT

This refers to your inquiry about a missing payment. If the payment is still missing, please complete the other side of this card and return it in the preaddressed envelope. No postage is needed.
NO FURTHER ACTION WILL BE TAKEN ON THE PAYMENT UNLESS THIS CARD IS COMPLETED, SIGNED, AND RETURNED.

If you receive the payment before you hear from the Treasury Department, please notify the Social Security Office.

Social Security Office

FINANCIAL ORGANIZATION

Name

Address

Zip Code

Routing and Transit Number

☐ If checking, or ☐ If savings   Depositor's Account Number

Form SSA-735 (3-84)

GPO : 1988 O – 214–194

Name of Payee to whom missing payment is due *(Please Print)*

Social Security Claim Number

DATE OF PAYMENT

Payment for: ☐ Social Security · ☐ Supplemental Security Income ☐ Black Lung

---

The above described payment was *(check applicable box)* →

☐ Not Received

Received, but (a) ☐ Destroyed ☐ Lost ☐ Stolen   (b) *Was it endorsed?* ☐ Yes ☐ No

ANYONE WHO MAKES A FALSE CLAIM COMMITS A CRIME PUNISHABLE UNDER FEDERAL LAW and can be FINED not more than $10,000 OR IMPRISONED not more than five years, OR BOTH. (Title 18 USCS, Sec. 287, U.S. Code)

Have you changed your mailing address ☐ YES ☐ NO

Current Mailing Address *(Include Zip Code)*

I/we wish to make formal claim to the Treasury Department for stoppage of payment and the issuance of a substitute payment. (Both husband and wife must sign if co-payees of a combined payment.) *(Please note information on reverse side.)*

SIGNATURE OF PAYEE

↑

Date

Payee's telephone number *(area code)*

SIGNATURE OF CO-PAYEE OR FINANCIAL ORGANIZATION REPRESENTATIVE

↑

Form SSA-725 (3-84)

APPENDIX 11

Effect of Marriage of One Beneficiary to Another
(see Sec. 904)

Type of Beneficiary	Effect of Marriage to Another Beneficiary
I. Retired Worker (Sec. 202) Disabled Worker (Sec. 203) Widow(er) (Sec. 207) Disabled Widow(er) (Sec. 209) Surviving Divorced Spouse (divorced widow(er)) (Sec. 210) Disabled Surviving Divorced Spouse (divorced widow(er)) (Sec. 210)	No effect, benefits continue
II. Divorced Spouse (Sec. 206) Parent (Sec. 215)	Benefits terminate if marriage is to a Retired or Disabled Worker, or a Child under 18 or in school; if marriage is to any other beneficiary, benefits continue.
III. Mother/Father (young widow(er)) (Sec. 208) Divorced Mother/Father (Sec. 210) Disabled Adult Child (Sec. 213)	Benefits terminate if marriage to a Child under 18 or in school (Child's benefits also terminate); if marriage is to any other beneficiary, benefits continue.
IV. Child under 18 or in School (Sec. Sec. 211-212)	Benefits terminate upon remarriage to anyone.

APPENDIX 12

Delayed Retirement Credits

The amount of a Delayed Retirement Credit is calculated as a percentage of the Primary Insurance Amount, based on the number of months no benefit is received after age sixty-five due to excess earnings. The percentages listed are annual. The credit for each month is $1/12$ of the annual figure. The amount of the credit is based on year of birth.

Year of Birth	Annual Credit
1917-24	3%
1925-26	3.5%
1927-28	4.0%
1929-30	4.5%
1931-32	5%
1933-34	5.5%
1935-36	6%
1937-38	6.5%
1939-40	7.0%
1941-42	7.5%
1943 and later	8.0%

APPENDIX 13

Medicare Premiums and Deductibles

Hospital Insurance	2001	2002
Premium—Part A	$300	$319 ($175 for those with 30–39 QC's)
Medical Insurance		
Premium—Part B	$50	$54
Hospital Insurance—Part A		
Co-Payments		
First 60 Days (Total)	$792	$812
61st-90th Day (per day)	$198	$203
Lifetime Reserve (per day)	$396	$406
Skilled Nursing Care		
20-100th day (per day)	$99	$101.50
Medical Insurance—Part B		
Yearly Deductible	$100	$100

INDEX

T

U

V

W

SPHINX® PUBLISHING ORDER FORM

TO:			SHIP TO:		
e #		Terms	F.O.B.	Chicago, IL	Ship Date

Charge my: ☐ VISA ☐ MasterCard ☐ American Express ☐ **Money Order or Personal Check**

Credit Card Number   **Expiration Date**

y	ISBN	Title	Retail
	SPHINX PUBLISHING NATIONAL TITLES		
___	1-57248-148-X	Cómo Hacer su Propio Testamento	$16.95
___	1-57248-147-1	Cómo Solicitar su Propio Divorcio	$24.95
___	1-57248-166-8	The Complete Book of Corporate Forms	$24.95
___	1-57248-163-3	Crime Victim's Guide to Justice (2E)	$21.95
___	1-57248-159-5	Essential Guide to Real Estate Contracts	$18.95
___	1-57248-160-9	Essential Guide to Real Estate Leases	$18.95
___	1-57248-139-0	Grandparents' Rights (3E)	$24.95
___	1-57248-188-9	Guia de Inmigración a Estados Unidos (3E)	$24.95
___	1-57248-187-0	Guia de Justicia para Victimas del Crimen	$21.95
___	1-57248-103-X	Help Your Lawyer Win Your Case (2E)	$14.95
___	1-57248-164-1	How to Buy a Condominium or Townhome (2E)	$19.95
___	1-57248-191-9	How to File Your Own Bankruptcy (5E)	$21.95
___	1-57248-132-3	How to File Your Own Divorce (4E)	$24.95
___	1-57248-100-5	How to Form a DE Corporation from Any State	$24.95
___	1-57248-083-1	How to Form a Limited Liability Company	$22.95
___	1-57248-099-8	How to Form a Nonprofit Corporation	$24.95
___	1-57248-133-1	How to Form Your Own Corporation (3E)	$24.95
___	1-57248-224-9	How to Form Your Own Partnership (2E)	$24.95
___	1-57248-119-6	How to Make Your Own Will (2E)	$16.95
___	1-57248-200-1	How to Register Your Own Copyright (4E)	$24.95
___	1-57248-104-8	How to Register Your Own Trademark (3E)	$21.95
___	1-57071-349-9	How to Win Your Unemployment Compensation Claim	$21.95
___	1-57248-118-8	How to Write Your Own Living Will (2E)	$16.95
___	1-57248-156-0	How to Write Your Own Premarital Agreement (3E)	$24.95
___	1-57248-158-7	Incorporate in Nevada from Any State	$24.95
___	1-57071-333-3	Jurors' Rights (2E)	$12.95
___	1-57071-400-2	Legal Research Made Easy (2E)	$16.95
___	1-57248-165-X	Living Trusts and Other Ways to Avoid Probate (3E)	$24.95

Qty	ISBN	Title	Retail
___	1-57248-186-2	Manual de Beneficios para el Seguro Social	$18.95
___	1-57248-220-6	Mastering the MBE	$16.95
___	1-57248-167-6	Most Valuable Bus. Legal Forms You'll Ever Need (3E)	$21.95
___	1-57248-130-7	Most Valuable Personal Legal Forms You'll Ever Need	$24.95
___	1-57248-098-X	The Nanny and Domestic Help Legal Kit	$22.95
___	1-57248-089-0	Neighbor v. Neighbor (2E)	$16.95
___	1-57248-169-2	The Power of Attorney Handbook (3E)	$19.95
___	1-57248-149-8	Repair Your Own Credit and Deal with Debt	$18.95
___	1-57248-168-4	The Social Security Benefits Handbook (3E)	$18.95
___	1-57071-399-5	Unmarried Parents' Rights	$19.95
___	1-57071-354-5	U.S.A. Immigration Guide (3E)	$19.95
___	1-57248-192-7	The Visitation Handbook	$18.95
___	1-57248-138-2	Winning Your Personal Injury Claim (2E)	$24.95
___	1-57248-162-5	Your Right to Child Custody, Visitation, and Support (2E)	$24.95
___	1-57248-157-9	Your Rights When You Owe Too Much	$16.95
	CALIFORNIA TITLES		
___	1-57248-150-1	CA Power of Attorney Handbook (2E)	$18.95
___	1-57248-151-X	How to File for Divorce in CA (3E)	$26.95
___	1-57071-356-1	How to Make a CA Will	$16.95
___	1-57248-145-5	How to Probate and Settle and Estate in CA	$26.95
___	1-57248-146-3	How to Start a Business in CA	$18.95
___	1-57071-358-8	How to Win in Small Claims Court in CA	$16.95
___	1-57248-196-X	The Landlord's Legal Guide in CA	$24.95
	FLORIDA TITLES		
___	1-57071-363-4	Florida Power of Attorney Handbook (2E)	$16.95
___	1-57248-176-5	How to File for Divorce in FL (7E)	$26.95
___	1-57248-177-3	How to Form a Corporation in FL (5E)	$24.95
___	1-57248-203-6	How to Form a Limited Liability Co. in FL (2E)	$24.95
___	1-57071-401-0	How to Form a Partnership in FL	$22.95

Form Continued on Following Page   **Subtotal** _____

SUBTOTAL THIS PAGE _____

SUBTOTAL PREVIOUS PAGE _____

Shipping — $5.00 for 1st book, $1.00 each additional _____

Illinois residents add 6.75% sales tax _____

Connecticut residents add 6.00% sales tax _____

TOTAL _____